Do You See What I See?

SERMONS FOR ADVENT, CHRISTMAS AND EPIPHANY

Do You See What I See?

SERMONS FOR ADVENT, CHRISTMAS AND EPIPHANY

**CYCLE B
FIRST LESSON TEXTS**

FRANK H. SEILHAMER

C.S.S. Publishing Co., Inc.
Lima, Ohio

DO YOU SEE WHAT I SEE?

Copyright © 1990 by
The C.S.S. Publishing Company, Inc.
Lima, Ohio

All rights reserved. No part of this publication may be reproduced, stored in a retrieval system, or transmitted in any form or by any means, electronic, mechanical, photocopying, recording, or otherwise, without the prior permission of the publisher. Inquiries should be addressed to: The C.S.S. Publishing Company, Inc., 628 South Main Street, Lima, Ohio 45804.

Library of Congress Cataloging-in-Publication Data

Seilhamer, Frank H.
  Do you see what I see? / by Frank Seilhamer.
      p.   cm.
  ISBN 1-55673-223-6
  1. Bible. O.T.--Sermons.   2. Sermons, American.   3. Advent sermons.   4. Christmas sermons.   5. Epiphany season--Sermons.
  6. Common lectionary.   I. Title
  BV40.S45 1990
  252'.61--dc20   90-34930
                                                                     CIP

9055 / ISBN 1-55673-223-6   PRINTED IN U.S.A.

To my Grandparents
Joseph and Mary Paravate
who were my unfailing providers of love,
understanding, acceptance and support
when I needed them most.

Contents

Introduction			9
Advent 1	Isaiah 63:16—64:8	Ready Redeemers, Steady Fathers and Advent!	13
Advent 2	Isaiah 40:1-11	Comfort, Deserts and Shepherds	21
Advent 3	Isaiah 61:1-4, 8-11	On Holy Ground	27
Advent 4	2 Samuel 7:8-16	Here, There and Everywhere!	35
The Nativity of Our Lord	Isaiah 9:2-7	The Light in the Darkness	43
Christmas 1	Isaiah 45:22-25	Gentle Jesus	51
Christmas 2	Isaiah 61:10—62:3	Getting Out of Your Own Way	61
The Baptism of Our Lord	Isaiah 42:1-7	Thank You, God, for Wanting Me!	71
Epiphany 2	1 Samuel 3:1-10 (11-20)	Do You Hear What I Hear?	81
Epiphany 3	Jonah 3:1-5, 10	Disciple-Makers On The Way	89
Epiphany 4	Deuteronomy 18:15-20	The Word of the Lord Came	99
Epiphany 5	Job 7:1-7	Keeping Up the Pitch	107
Epiphany 6	2 Kings 5:1-14	What Do You Do When the Raft Comes Apart?	115
Epiphany 7	Isaiah 43:18-25	The Now and Yet is What to Be	123
Epiphany 8	Hosea 2:14-20	When the Wheels Fall Off of Your Life	131
The Transfiguration of Our Lord	2 Kings 2:1-12a	"Help! Help! Help!"	139

Introduction

Anyone who reads the Old Testament with care cannot fail to see that for those who experience what is recorded there, passed it on by word of mouth, wrote it down and thereby transmitted it to us, God is no far-off deity! The God of the Old Testament is neither worshiped at a distance, nor operative in his universe only as an impersonal "principle." He is a God who is personally and continually in touch with human beings right where they live. That is why the Lessons from these texts throb with a sense of the nearness of God. In them the Lord speaks to his people, walks with them, leads them, and at times chastens them. While "Holy," and in many ways "Other," he is a God who has his feet "on the ground" that he created. He always is where people are rather than spinning around the spheres in splendid isolation!

Because this is so, for some religions and individuals the Old Testament can "stand on its own" as God's full revelation of himself. Love, mercy, forgiveness, righteousness, compassion, loyalty, justice and all other attributes and characteristics which God has to demonstrate in his interaction with his creation and creatures are to be found in its pages. Moreover, they are there full-blown, not as mere "shadows" of what is to come at some later date. That is why it is possible for non-Christians to study, meditate upon, teach and preach about God from those texts without reference to anything else other than life, past, present and future.

But for Christians that is not possible. Though it is incumbent upon us to treat the Old Testament with integrity, giving it its original frames of reference without making it into a string of "proof texts" for our particular theological perspectives, we cannot read its pages without taking into account Jesus Christ. As St. John so powerfully framed the issue:

> *In the beginning was the Word, and the Word was with God, and the Word was God. He was in the beginning with God; all things were made through him, and without him was not anything made that was made. In him was life, and the life was the light of men . . . . And the Word became flesh and dwelt among us, full of grace and truth; we have beheld his glory, glory as of the only Son of the Father.* (John 1:1-4, 14)

Since that revelation the Christian community can no longer touch the Old Testament, read its prophecies, be moved with its calls to repentance, faith, obedience, acceptance of God's love and forgiveness, and promises of new days and ages to come, without seeing and sensing in them the Carpenter from Nazareth. As Martin Luther pointed out, *Christ is the heart of God's self-revelation:*

> *He is the center from which the entire circle has been drawn and toward which it looks . . . and when viewed aright all stories in the Holy Scripture refer to Christ.*

The sermons that follow reflect that perspective. Though they begin with the settings and words given by the Prophets in their time and place, Jesus' ministry, mission and teaching constantly appear. No apologies are made for that fact. My training in the fields of Old Testament, Semitic and Near Eastern studies and languages always leads me to listen to the Old Testament with care, love, anticipation and wonder. But I cannot shut out what I have seen and experienced of God in the "Word made flesh."

The Old and New Testaments are parts of one continuous revelation from God. They are forever intertwined for the Christian.

Because that is so, Christian preaching can never cease to be shaped and guided by that fact if it is to remain true to Jesus' Great Commission:

> *Go therefore and make disciples of all nations, baptizing them in the name of the Father and of the Son and of the Holy Spirit, teaching them to observe all that I have commanded you; and lo, I am with you always, to the close of the age.*[1]
> (Matthew 28:19-20)

To that ever-present Lord, Father, Son, and Holy Spirit, be honor and glory forever and ever!

---

[1] *Luther's Werke,* Weimar, Vol. 47, p. 66, translation by Frank H. Seilhamer.

Ready Redeemers, Steady Fathers and Advent!

Advent 1   *Isaiah 63:16—64:8*

"Stir up your power, O Lord, and come . . ." are the words from the Collect that has served as the "opener" for Advent for hundreds of years. What has kept it coming from the mouths of the faithful is that it captures, clean and simple, the longing of every believing heart. When we are in trouble, or lonely, or at wit's end, we want to get God to "stir up his power, and come!"

Isaiah had the same hunger beating in his breast.

> O that thou wouldst rend the heavens
>   and come down,
> that the mountains might quake at
>   thy presence —
> as when the fire kindles brushwood
>   and the fire causes water to boil . . . .
>
> From of old no one has heard
> or perceived by the ear,
>   no eye has seen a God besides thee,
> who works for those who wait for
>   him.

Do You See What I See?

What a rousing call that is to a God loaded with fire-power and a track record of hearing and helping! And when you add to that the parental cast he gives to that sensitive deity . . .

> O LORD, thou art our Father;
> we are the clay, and thou art our
>   potter;
> we are all the work of thy hand . . .

. . . you can understand even better the staying power of our Advent Collect. God is drawn there as a Father, a being, mind you, a passionate Creator. For the Lord of Isaiah's plea, or the Collect's cry, is not an isolated "It," nor a disembodied intellectual "Principle." Both link us up with a Holy God who is "Heavenly," above and over all . . . a God who, as such, *could appear remote and out of reach* . . . but a God *who at the same time is a "Father."* He stands on this turf with us, within earshot of our needs. He is a God who is as close to us as our earthly kin.

The member of the family to whom both the Old and New Testaments liken God is one who sparked the process that produced us originally, and who cared for and protected us from that moment until now. When they call Him "Father" they bring into the fore a tender, yet strong, name, especially in their own culture. It is a term that can evoke a warm and affectionate feeling of trust on the part of those who hear and use it.

For most people, "Father" is that extraordinary being who possesses the power to be one of the greatest shapers of the lives he generates and touches. A *good* father is one who uses these powers positively and carefully, putting his family's welfare ahead of his own. He gives support and encouragement, and a secure base, for the growth of the children who are his. He is the one to whom we can turn in time of need, knowing in advance that we will get a hearing. Whatever is right and available will be given to get life back on the right track, and with his help and encouragement the big problems have the possibility of being made small.

Fathers like that become the models for their sons' lives. Their daughters often see in them the qualities they will want in their own husbands, and later in their children. So when the Bible holds up that word to describe God, it describes the relationship that is

Advent, Christmas, and Epiphany

to exist between the pray-er and the one prayed to as one filled with the enormous promise of intimacy, acceptance and help.

But that term "Father" has a dangerous flip-side to it. It can be a tricky, negative and frightening word as well. Isaiah's own people, when they used it in reference to God, did so carefully and with caution because of the potential abuse it carried with it.

Pagans in ancient Samaria used it three thousand years before the Christian era to describe the gods they worshiped. Later, the Canaanites, among whom Abraham, Isaac and Jacob lived, and who later become the neighbors of the people of Israel when they were freed from Pharaoh's bondage, used the term as well. Among those foreigners the gods often were viewed as fertility figures, whose worship gave rise to temple prostitution and sexual license among their disciples. The image of the gods the Canaanites worshiped, while addressed as "father," was that of an immortal dictator who demanded from his followers often enormous tribute to buy his favors. The prices he extracted for the people to be accepted and helped often included the life of at least one of the worshiper's children. It was usually the first born that had to be sacrificed for this "father" to bestow a blessing.

This extractor of a god was something like the bandit my grandfather met shortly after he landed in the United States from Italy. Nineteen years old, unable to speak English and desperate for a job, he was told that if he was to get a position he had to visit the head of a family that controlled many of the jobs in the city of Pittsburgh. When my grandfather walked into the room, the old man asked him what gifts he had brought for him. "If I had the money to buy you gifts I wouldn't need your help to find a job," the youngster answered. "Stupido," "stupid," "Non gratio," "ingrate," the old man roared. Then he had the young immigrant thrown out on his ear. No payment, no help, is how it was in little Italy . . . and in Canaan, even with those prayed to as "father!"

And with some human fathers it is that way still. Utter the word "father" and some people feel pain, and resentment, and fear. For some of us "father" brings back experiences of abuse and terror at the hands of people who made our lives hellish nightmares.

What if your father was a drunk, or a heavy-handed persecutor? What if he abused you sexually, or was a vindictive down-dragger who tried his best to destroy your confidence and self-respect? What if he made you spend your formative years wondering if he would abandon you, or if you would eat or have a roof over your head for long? How would you relate to that word "Father" even when it is applied to God?

I deal regularly with people who have fled, and are still fleeing years later, on foot or emotionally, from such earthly fathers. They have to struggle with this dark side of that word so many people love. And yet when Jesus came and reached out to people who were bruised and battered, he saw the same face on God that Isaiah did:

> "... What man of you, if his son asks him for bread, will give him a stone? Or if he asks for a fish, will give him a serpent? If you then, who are evil, know how to give good gifts to your children, how much more will your father who is in heaven give good gifts to those who ask him?" (Matthew 7:9-11)

"When you look toward your Father, who is in heaven," Jesus is saying, "I tell you He is an awesome, tender, loyal life-giver to whom you can trustingly turn your heart and face."

In the Aramaic, Jesus' native tongue, and the one in which he undoubtedly spoke to his disciples about God as Father, the word used was "Abba." And that was the name Jesus himself applied to God when he reached out for him at some of the most intimate and trying moments of his life. "Abba" is not a formal title used by adults in addressing the one who sired him or her. "Abba" is the toddler's term, the first word said by an infant when it finally recognizes its parent. "Daddy" is the most accurate rendering of the word Jesus used for God in the opening burst of this prayer. Unsophisticated and exuberant, there it stands, conjuring up a picture of a child rushing up to a loved one with complete abandon, leaping and throwing himself into a pair of arms he is certain will catch him up in safety.

There is no caution in that term, "Abba!" No sense of playing it safe to see if he is ready, or in the mood, to give you his attention! Embedded in the word is the promise that that Father, our Father, is a God who is eternally "there" for us.

In the midst of all that is changing and phoney in so much of the world we live in day after day, that promise that the passage from Isaiah holds out to us is priceless. Like anything else so out of step with life as it usually operates, we wonder if it will hold up when tested. One of the most haunting fears with which we have to contend is that of being betrayed or abandoned by those we trusted. Not only have I felt that in my own life, but I have seen it up close in so many others that I have stopped counting the cases.

The life of one such tragic person with whom I worked was shredded by such an experience. In his mid-thirties at the time he came to me, he was having trouble keeping a marriage together, and had been struggling for years with long bouts of insomnia that sapped his strength. He was not able to make friendships that lasted for more than a few weeks or months. He was always looking for the moment when anyone close to him would turn their backs and walk away.

I finally learned that at the bottom of his distress was an experience he had had when he was six years old. His mother and father had taken him and his younger sister to his grandparents' home on a Friday evening. After dinner his parents had put them both to bed and tucked them in. They told them they were going for groceries and would be there when they woke up in the morning to take them home again.

When the parents left the room, the youngsters hopped out of bed and watched from the window as they got into the car. The car door slammed shut. The auto pulled away . . . never to return again. It was nearly eleven years later when a letter arrived telling how the parents had felt trapped, and had wanted no kids to take care of. That young man had never seen his father and mother again from that night until I met him.

And yet, every time he heard a car door close, even as an adult, it would wake him up, or an urge to get to his feet would hit him. It was all he could do to keep from running to a window to see if his parents had come back. If *they* could abandon him, their own flesh and blood, wouldn't *everybody else* eventually do it, too?

All sorts of human beings have learned in their experiences with him that God, the "heavenly Father" of the Prayer, is the Holy "Other." He is One who will not let go of those who are his.

Do You See What I See?

> *Call upon me in the day of trouble and I will deliver you. . . .*
> *he promised to his people.*   (Psalm 50:15)

> *"He heard my voice and my cry (when) the clutches of*
> *death wrapped around me.*
>   *From the brink of destruction he pulled me back;*
> *dried off my tears and kept me from collapsing . . ."*
>   (Psalm 116:1b, 8)

Though some human beings may back off when the ante is high, not this "heavenly Father" . . . not this "Abba" of a God, Isaiah is saying. This Father who:

> *to make thy name known to thy*
>   *adversaries,*
>   *. . . that the nations might tremble*
>   *at thy presence!*
>   *. . . didst terrible things which*
>   *we looked not for,*
> *[who when He] came down, the mountains*
>   *quaked at thy presence*

is one who carries you in his arms like a baby, regardless of your age.

Even though:

> *Behold, thou wast angry, and we*
>   *sinned;*
> *in our sins we have been a long time,*
>   *and shall we be saved?*
> *We have all become like one who is*
>   *unclean,*
> *and all our righteous deeds are like a*
>   *polluted garment.*
> *We all fade like a leaf,*
>   *and our iniquities, like the wind,*
>   *take us away . . .*

 · He has surrounded you with his heart, and will not let you go. That being so, he will never let you out of his sight!

Advent, Christmas, and Epiphany

Little children too young to speak, still learning what an earthly parent is, are scooped up and held in those arms of his. Youth, caught up in the struggle to become "themselves," and trying to find some "space," he has hold of, too. New parents, struggling to hack house payments, build a career or careers, and caringly mold a family, and middle-agers and middle-agers-plus, whose hair is grey, or gone, and who are trying just to survive . . . all have his undivided attention, as wild and incredible as that sounds!

You name the problem, or the opportunity, the anxiety or frustration, and "our Father" is the one who casts the shadow that provides the shade that shelters us from the heat of life's most trying moments. He is that close and that caring! Isaiah at another moment said it this way:

> *But now thus says the Lord,*
> *he who created you O Jacob,*
> *he who formed you, O Israel:*
> *"Fear not, for I have redeemed you;*
> *I have called you by name, you are mine.*
> *When you pass through the waters, I will be*
>   *with you;*
> *and through the rivers, they shall not*
>   *overwhelm you;*
> *when you walk through the fire you shall not be*
>   *burned,*
> *and the flame shall not consume you.*
> *For I am the Lord your God,*
>   *the Holy One of Israel, your Savior."*
>   (Isaiah 43:1-3)

And God has made those promises to you, and to me, as well. The point is that the One who is "our Father," and who holds us in his arms, is the Holy One who has the awesome power to deliver whatever it is that he sees we need!

The best-meaning earthly fathers don't have that power at their command. Though they can stand beside us through thick and thin, there comes a time for us, and for them, when their strength and resources, and life itself, run out. When that happens, all they can do is stand by and watch, or close their eyes and leave us alone when their last breath is taken. Even fathers who seem bigger than life, and somehow indestructible, really aren't. And when they go, their departure can be devastating!

But having a God whose arms are wrapped around us, and feeling the security of his power and nearness, starts prying loose the clammy fingers of fear and hopelessness that make us feel that there will be no dawn, no chance for a new tomorrow. That is the truly miraculous power which this Lord of ours has. When others collapse and fade away, he remains intact. As the *eternal One,* he can take us with him through the twists and turns and snarls of this world, until at last he delivers us safely home . . . where we will never feel separated from him who willed that we should have life in the first place.

It is to this God, this eternal, ready Redeemer, this waiting "Father," that we cry in this season of Advent, "Stir up your power, O Lord, and come." And knowing that he will do precisely that, like Isaiah, we wait for His appearing,

    confidently . . .

        and eagerly . . .

            and with a joyful heart!

Comforts, Deserts and Shepherds

Advent 2 *Isaiah 40:1-11*

Advent is traditionally ushered in with a giant wreath encircled with four candles. The flames on those tapers brighten the future, while at the same time they consume the wax and wicks which kindled the light. So, the flaming tapers on the wreath signal the ending of one dimension of existence as they illuminate the way for the arrival of fresh opportunities.

The abiding message they leave is that the two, *death and birth*, go hand in hand. That isn't the note we prefer to set the tone of a season like this one. Advent, leading to Christmas, with its carols of joy, and the good cheer, ought not to have any such gloomy clouds hovering on the horizon, don't you agree? And yet, if you listen to many of the lessons that are read in these four weeks preceding Christmas, you will hear proclamations of warnings, and the promises of strength and comfort woven in among them.

The words of Isaiah, read just a moment ago, reveal the distinctive Advent mix:

> *A voice says, "Cry!" And I said, "What shall I cry?" All flesh is grass, and all its beauty is like the flowers of the field. The grass withers, the flower fades, when the breath of the LORD blows upon it; surely the people is grass. The grass withers, the*

Do You See What I See?

> *flower fades; but the word of our God will stand for ever. Get you up to a high mountain, O Zion, herald of good tidings; lift up your voice with strength, O Jerusalem, herald of good tidings, lift it up, fear not; say to the cities of Judah, "Behold your God!" Behold, the Lord GOD comes with might, and his arm rules for him; behold, his reward is with him, and his recompense before him. He will feed his flock like a shepherd, he will gather the lambs in his arms, he will carry them in his bosom, and gently lead those that are with young.*

A powerful and beautiful passage, it has the Good news/Bad news theme running right through the heart of it. The *bad news* is that there are few things in life that last, including people! "All flesh is grass, and all its beauty is like the flower of the field. The grass withers, the flower fades, when the breath of the LORD blows upon it." The *good news* is that God will come to remedy that situation. "Behold, the Lord God comes with might, and his arm rules for him; behold, his reward is with him . . . ." The bad news is that sometimes when He comes it is with a *vengeance* . . . "his recompense [is] before him." The good news is that even then He is a God with the kind of passion that makes Him a "carer" of the first Order . . . "He will feed his flock like a shepherd, he will gather the lambs in his arms."

If you are like I am, those last words sound good to you. We want God to come running to us all right, but when you and I are ready . . . and in the "good news" mode! Who doesn't want him when he's coming in a super mood, and packing gifts! But what about the bad news days Isaiah points his finger to like the "Spirit of Christmas Yet to Come" did for Scrooge . . . when God seems to be hovering about in a vengeful mode?

There are times like that. You know it full well . . . tough times that can make any of us wilt and sag. Within the last few days I have sat with people who find themselves under the shadow of despair at the very time when our Christmas decorations are going up just about everywhere we look. A fellow whose job has suddenly evaporated, a middle-aged couple one of whose fading health has taken a real nose-dive, a young family sent to me by a local agency to help get their finances, as well as their lives, together so that they can keep their marriage and their children intact. With

Advent, Christmas, and Epiphany

their worlds in a turmoil struggling through their personal deserts, they are only the nearest members of the "wilderness" pilgrims.

Today our *children* grow up experiencing depression because they feel there is no future for them in a world they expect to see destroyed before they reach adulthood. The new warming of relationships between East and West may have eased the anxieties for many of us, but who knows how it will all end? Hopes have been raised then dashed before, many times. Who can tell if we can emerge from them without an international explosion in some place or other?

A Baltimore psychiatrist has coined the label "nuclearosis" to identify and explain it. These children's anxiety and loss of hope often gives rise to their push to "do it now." And that can lead to everything from grade school drug experimentation to teen-aged suicide. Before many of them have reached their twenties they *have* done it all. They have burned out and died inside, and see little reason to hold out, let alone sacrifice, for a tomorrow that may never come.

And you can see the wilderness syndrome in the faces of some of our *older ones*. What value is a future that stretches on if you have to exist in fear of out-living your resources, or even your "welcome" to remain alive. With the anxiety about Social Security that may run out, or a life's savings going, and aches and pains dominating most conscious moments, where is the beauty of old age that someone told them there would be? *60 Minutes* laid out for the general public recently a fact I had realized a number of years ago . . . growing numbers of our elderly are ending their own lives because living on is too loaded with "bad news."

And it erodes those of us in the *middle years*, too! On some mornings doesn't it seem that *The New Yorker* cartoon of a frazzled salesman in his manager's office, really sums it up? Sitting at his desk the boss looks up at the sagging fellow standing in front of him, chin on his chest, belly hanging over his belt, collar open and tie in disarray: "So it's a dog fight. Just see to it that you bite faster than the other dogs!"

Where are all of the fruits of *your* tussle? Are your kids out in the world making you proud, with at least a few rungs on the ladder of success under foot? Or are you one of those who have been out-fought, sitting with the tatters of your dreams, your situation out of control, maybe frighteningly so?

Yes, indeed, these are the real dry lands and the wilderness, as threatening as anything that the Hebrews met! The problem is that there seems to be nothing you can do about it. And yet it is just at this juncture of gloom that Isaiah calls out, "God can lift the load!" And he follows up by telling us how he can pull it off!

The first crack he opens in the pessimism is letting you know that God is making his way through your desert, and that he cares about what is going on, even if he is not responding at the moment like you think he should!

> *Behold, the lord GOD comes with might, and his arm rules for him; behold, his reward is with him, and his recompense is before him.*

That word "come" Isaiah employs is double-edged. It is the Hebrew *bo*. It draws the picture of an individual arriving personally on the scene, ready to help those whose needs he came to meet, or whose call prompted him to hurry to their side. It is a term that has built into it the promise that the God who is arriving is coming ready to get involved in what it is that ails us.

Its second dimension is that he is not planning to leave until he has laid the plans for the ultimate remedying of the challenge that the desert laid on us! Like a shepherd unwilling to abandon his flock, "he will gather the lambs in his arms, he will carry them in his bosom, and gently lead those that are with young." These wrap-up lines in the passage have the prophet falling all over himself trying to tell us in the midst of our depression to "get ready for great things to begin."

From the vantage point of folks at their wit's end, Isaiah must seem like a P. R. man from a president in a time of depression saying "Buck-up" when you can hear the sound of the avalanche already coming! He would have you believe that full recovery is just a wink away! And, like those ancient Israelites, we have gotten so used to that sort of chicanery that we put our tongues in cheek pretty fast.

Advent, Christmas, and Epiphany

But in fact Isaiah's words became a footer on which the New Testament was to build its unforgettable definition of faith, that it is: "the assurance of things hoped for, the conviction of things not seen." (Hebrews 11:1)

"Assurance," a promise given by someone you trust that what he or she says will happen. *"Hoped for . . . ,"* that which goes beyond normal expectation. *"Conviction . . . ,"* an opinion based on past performance, like a lawyer laying the evidence before the jury and asking them to decide a case. *"Not seen . . . ,"* a situation that has not come to hand as yet. But like Isaiah, the writer of Hebrews pushes us to recall how we were in situations in the past when we thought we were finished . . . abandoned . . . hopeless . . . and God pulled us through to see this moment. Remember? And what God did then he can do again. What is more, he is promising to do just that!

This leap of faith is what God calls for. It is not a leap into you know not what. It is a leap into the arms of One who can carry the universe without raising a sweat, the One for whom all things really are possible!

But what sounds easy often can be excruciatingly difficult . . . even when it comes to trusting God. We can't just close our eyes in the face of pain and loss and failure and say, "Go away!" because we were told to do it that way. *Trust* is *work* because it involves hanging on with all our might, like a person hanging on to a ledge with the street far below, waiting for help to arrive when the fingers get numb, and the body says, "Let go!" What Isaiah understood was that the strength to hang on comes from *remembering* what God did to get you this far.

A friend of mine was a prisoner of war in North Korea. A brutal regime, his captors nearly killed him with torture and starvation. When not being questioned, he was locked in solitary confinement, with no other friendly human being with whom to relate. To keep his sanity, he hit on the idea of building a house for him and his wife in his head as he sat in his cell. For hours on end he would stare at a wall and draw in his mind the details he one day would build in fact. Down to the smallest piece of trim, he plotted it out to keep his mind alert and his hope burning. "I hung on and survived," he told me, "by taking it a little bit at a time."

Do You See What I See?

What he did is marvelous advice for all of us in dealing with our deserts. Take it a little at a time. We can become overwhelmed trying to imagine what is going to happen next week, next month, or next year, or even tomorrow. Jesus said to take *all of life,* including the bad days, in *day-tight compartments.* Like walking . . . it is only the next step that we can take anyway. Whatever the kind of "exile" it is that we feel, the longest journey is made up of just a series of next steps. A better day is coming because God says it is. And it is he, not us, who has the height and vantage point to see toward what lies ahead.

In the play *Camelot,* Merlin tells Arthur how he and the young king differ. Arthur lives in the *now* fearing the *unknown future,* while as a magiciain Merlin lives in the *now having been into the future already.* "I live backwards," Merlin says to Arthur. "Because of that while you grow old, I youthen."

Like Arthur, as our years pile up, the burdens we pick up seem eventually to overtax our strengths. And life can appear to be a desert, a wilderness, through which we will never be able to pass. But God, who has the future in his scope, as well as the present and the past, seems to stay young . . . and strong enough to handle, and hoist, and haul, and lift us over, whatever it is that can weigh us down, or even floor us! When he decides the time is to act he will come, as Isaiah promised, into our desert, and do it "with a vengeance!" "He will come and save us."

He still stands *beside us* when everything outside says that he has vanished. And *he waits there* to pull us into eternal security when the right moment to do it ticks out. That is the truth of the matter. Yet God doesn't march to the beat we drum; this also is the truth of the matter . . . he didn't go to all that trouble of giving us life, and traipsing through it with us this far, to go and dump us now!

That is what God was saying to the people of Israel in that call of Isaiah's that cut through the gloom like a blast . . . "Comfort, comfort my people . . . ." Despite all there was to be down-hearted about, a great day was coming. And that is the same message he has for you and me on this December day: ". . . lift up your voice with strength . . . lift it up, fear not," . . . and hang tough!

On Holy Ground

Advent 3   *Isaiah 61:1-4, 8-11*

The magazine, *Partners*, published by the Evangelical Lutheran Church in America, and sent to all of its pastors, dedicated an entire issue to the subject of preaching. It was designed, I suspect, as a multipurpose piece . . . to tell us tactfully that the current state of sermons needs immediate attention . . . and to give us some hints and helps about how to do them better!

Sitting with the journal in my hands the week it came, my mind went spinning back to when that subject was underlined for me on a night thirty-two years ago. My head filled up with the rerun of my ordination service in June, 1959. Fixed before me was the moment at about 8:15 p.m., when, as I knelt on the steps before the altar with the hands of a Bishop, my pastor, and my major Professor from the Seminary on my head, these words were said as both a declaration and a prayer of consecration:

> *Almighty God, who has chosen you to be his minister, enable you to fulfill by his help what you have begun by his favor.*
>
> *Take thou the authority to preach the pure Word of God, and to administer the Holy Sacraments in the Church.*

Do You See What I See?

Then, as I knelt there, the Bishop read the passage from Isaiah you heard a couple of minutes ago . . .

> *he has anointed [you] to bring good tidings to the afflicted . . .*
> *to bind up the broken hearted . . .*
> *to proclaim liberty to the captives . . .*
> *to proclaim the year of the Lord's favor,*
> *and the day of vengeance of our God . . .*

What those words did was open my eyes to see, in a way I never had before, the awesomeness of the task that was being branded into my heart. They underlined for me for life what a staggering responsibility it would be, and still is, for me and people like me, to step into a pulpit to which the Spirit of God has pointed, and to be a channel for the Lord to reach out his hand to do those things of which Isaiah spoke, to, and for, individuals like you.

To many observers the act of preaching may look like nothing more than a person, with a fist full of notes and maybe a text from the Bible, standing up to give some weekly religious advice. Outwardly, I suppose, at least most of the time, we appear to be calm and assured, and what we have to say may even sound cut and dried!

Let me tell you that, at least for me, that is not the way it is! What is going on inside of me is something vastly different. Every time I step up here, and into places like it, my heart races, and I am overcome with a sense of awe about the whole event . . . .

My "inners" are filled with butterflies on the wing . . .
beads of perspiration start to pop into view . . .
and I usually wish someone else were here,
and I were where you are!

For I know that this is holy ground, and that the moment I stand here is a sacred one. In the following few minutes God is going to be, through me, present and speaking to you.

As a prophet, Isaiah knew that when he spoke to Israel.
Though *he* stood before them . . .
though *he* opened his mouth . . .
though the voice heard was *Isaiah's* . . .
it was, in fact, *God* who would be present to make *his* point.

Advent, Christmas, and Epiphany

When he wrote that: "The Spirit of the Lord is upon me," he was declaring that God, literally, was "putting him on!" When his appointee set out to do his bidding, God had the power, and used it, to take over people and use them as a "front" for communicating with others.

God did that with the man named Gideon back in the time of the Judges. (Chapters 6-8) With the Israelites under the oppression of the marauding bands of Midianites, God needed a leader to rally his people for a battle for their independence. Finding at last a cooperative, if a "look before you leap" type of human colleague, the Bible says that the Spirit of the Lord "took Gideon" (Judges 6:34) and used him as the rallying point for the victories that were won.

The word used in Hebrew for the English "took," is *lavesh*. It means "to put on like a garment." That is, when God co-opted Gideon for the task, *he dressed himself in his partner's body* and personally led the nation to triumph! What looked like Gideon was the Lord himself among his own. He made his approach to the people at hand in a form they could "tolerate" without being "blown away." That is why God used human beings to become his masks. He made the person whose faculties he used his "facade," regardless of the level of skill that they had before his co-opting.

God still does the same thing, and with folks as flawed as I am. When he calls me to speak, he is here in this place, putting me to use for his purposes. What I speak is the vehicle for the voice of God.

That does not mean that every word I utter is his, that every gesture is his, that each idea that I launch has been dictated by him! But, through these words, in the very act of preaching, God himself comes to you and me, and is active in this very place at this very instant. Wrapped in the words which my mouth sounds is something he wants you, or someone here, to have laid within his or her heart. For the "Spirit of the Lord is upon me," *me* too . . . the partial and fallible *me,* that he has sent out to do his proclaiming!

That is why sermons are serious business. Usually they are burdens, like babies, that it is a relief to have "delivered." Preachers must cultivate themselves, prepare themselves, to be the best tools God can have at his disposal. When that is done then we must watch to see what God will accomplish through us, and see what he will do for, and to, all who hear.

How I love it when God uses these minutes, and me, to deliver news that uplifts and soothes! I love to be used to give "garlands instead of ashes," and rub in the "oil of gladness," just as you like to have them delivered. What I have learned repeatedly in my ministry is how much people need those two gifts. The tragedy of life is that most people have neither. They think less of themselves and their potential, rather than more, than they should. Most folks with whom I come into contact are much too down on themselves.

Mothers and fathers come into my office with their faces and hearts dragging, convinced that they are the biggest failures that ever were given those roles. Children sit slouched over because they are sure that they have failed in so many things so often that they will never get anything in their lives in order for long. People beat themselves to pulps emotionally, and condemn themselves mercilessly for mistakes. And they are positive that God is as unrelenting in his appraisal of them and their chances to change as they are.

In his day Luther was nearly crushed by that same tendency in his own life. His view was of a God who was forever demanding the impossible from people, and condemning them for not performing it. I think the problem now is that most of us have reversed the roles. We are the ones who are unrelenting on ourselves, as well as others.

I have my hardest times convincing many people I see that they need to give up their self-hatred, and self-crucifixion, because God wants them to hear his words of forgiveness and assurance and confidence, and get on with making more of their todays and tomorrows than they may have made of their yesterdays. To do that they need to learn to love themselves as the Lord who made them does.

One of the techniques I use with those who seek my help is to have them make lists of things that are troubling them, what it is they would need to have to make the future ideal, and what they have going for them that can make what they desire to change come to be. It nearly always is that last list, what they have going for them, what is good about them, what talents and plus factors

Advent, Christmas, and Epiphany

in their personal make up, that is the hardest one for them to write down. Why? Maybe because they think, or have been taught that, that is "proud," or "arrogant," or "blowing their own horn." Christianity condemns any such self-appreciation, right? Wrong!

If Jesus meant it when he commanded the disciples to "love their neighbors as themselves," (Matthew 19:19) invoking the tradition of the ancient Israelites in the Book of Leviticus, (19:18) then he recognized the necessity of *loving oneself* as a *prerequisite* to moving on to love anybody else! If you *hate* yourself, and then treat others as you do yourself, you and I can be downright dangerous and destructive! It is our doing *that* which makes for so much of the havoc that is wrecked everywhere we look.

Self-hate makes us . . .

> jealous of others' achievements because they look too good and show what failures we are by comparison, making us feel even worse about ourselves than we did . . .
>> refuse to forgive the ones who hurt us because we cannot accept forgiveness ourselves, we "raunchy rats," because we are too worthless to be set free no matter what anybody says, even God . . .
>>> take the hardest, most demanding line with even those closest to us, *especially* those *closest* to us, because if we don't demand and threaten, they will never do what is needed and right . . .

and *we get cynical about all of existence,* until life becomes a treadmill of unrelenting drudgery with no light, or dawning, to which we can look forward!

It is no wonder suicides are rocketing as ways out of this morass! Why not end it, since we are wrecks waiting to be towed off and scrapped anyway. We deserve no better. No one, nowhere, has any reason to care about, or pull for, us in our dilemmas. We deserve the "dust of life."

Tough as it is, Isaiah tells those of us anointed by the Lord,

> *Bring good tidings to the afflicted . . .*
> *give them a garland instead of ashes . . .*

even though we resist the gift.

Do You See What I See?

Remember: God loves us . . . and who are we to tell him that he is wrong in thinking we are not worth his gift. Now *that* is arrogant!

Remember: God made us with the power and vision to bring the universe to heel . . . and if he wove that potential into the fabric of our lives, there it remains, no matter how dirty we may have gotten the linen!

Remember: God told us not to be paralyzed with fear for the future . . . concerned at times, maybe, but not panic-stricken or hopeless . . . because even in the valley of the shadow of death . . . he is with us!

Remember: we can burn the I.O.U.s we hold on each other because God has promised to burn all of ours that Jesus has signed for, and that is all of them.

Be free . . . and be a freedom-giver . . . put the role of Jailer, and grudge-tender into mothballs!

And that was my answer to a couple I had in my office one afternoon telling me that they were going to transfer to another denomination because they "never heard the Gospel or the Bible being preached" here! "You do not spend enough time holding sinners guilty and under the judgment of God." They are among those folks who somehow must feel that regular sermonic beatings are the cure for what ails them! If Isaiah is an accurate describer of what preaching is about, then the time one spends in lining out the "positive" dimensions of what news God has sent us to deliver is a good clue about whether or not we are doing what God commissioned us to do.

But, sometimes, in the sermons God *does come* to rebuke. He uses us to deliver sermons that "belt" people where it hurts the most, and where they want him to touch them the least. What he says in the ordination sermon of Jeremiah (1:10) about his preaching also is true for the rest of us as well. Preaching is two-fold:

to pluck up and to break down;
to destroy and to overthrow;
to build and to plant.

Advent, Christmas, and Epiphany

When the first of these dimensions come, and I dislike preaching them, they set folks to squirming, and sometimes to rebelling. I have people, occasionally, leave a service vowing under their breaths never to come back to hear something like that again! And in their discomfort I have understood how they felt. I have "been there" for sermons like that, too . . . when I suspected that the preacher had been "laying for me." I felt that he was undressing me in public, and hanging my linen out to dry. And I have held my breath until he finished for fear he would wrap up the darned thing by pointing to me and saying, "There sits the man!"

What made me feel that way, of course, was that what he was saying was the truth! The shoe that was being held out fit our foot, and that was not so because the preacher had targeted me, nor I anyone in particular, for a blast on that occasion. God had come to speak to some needy heart a word they needed to hear. On that occasion that heart happened to be mine, or yours. What I have learned to do when that happens is not get up in a huff. As painful as it can be to hear it, we need to thank God for caring enough about what happens to us to come right up to our sides to declare it. Like the poster in my office tells me and others who are willing to learn from it:

> *"The truth will make you free — but first it will make you miserable."*

The truth he speaks is not intended to "do us in." The reason God speaks it to us is to diagnose an illness that can kill us if left unattended.

If we went to a physician, and she told us we had heartburn when we really were experiencing a coronary, and she did it because she did not want to alarm us, or get us angry because of the news she gave us, would she be the kind of person to whom you would want to entrust your life? She might be "kindly," telling you what you hoped she would say when you pulled into her parking lot. But she would in fact be a killer from whom you had better run if you want to survive.

And there are times when God comes to put his finger on the sore spots in your life, and mine. When he does, resolve to take his diagnosis to heart . . . and change . . . and love him all the more for the caring.

Do You See What I See?

    How happy I am that most of the time God calls us to be his vehicles for *uplifting* and *strengthening*. Preaching, understood in its biblical sense, is *always positive!* Even when God speaks to us in "diagnoses," it is because he has come to us to bring his cure. In those moments when he puts his foot to worthless debris in our lives, he does it as the Re-Creator, coming to our aid.

    So . . . giving "garlands instead of ashes" . . .
        "the oil of gladness instead of mourning" . . .
            "the mantle of praise instead of a faint spirit" . . .
        as well as warnings of "the day of vengeance of our
        God" . . . for those who will have none of the others, what a marvelous task that is to have God lay upon a human being! Every time I step into this holy place, pray for me that I may keep myself open and ready for him to do that for your well-being, and for mine!

Here, There and Everywhere!

Advent 4   2 Samuel 7:8-16

> **Built** on a Rock the church dost stand
>   even when steeples are falling.
> Tumbled have spires in every land
>   bells still are chiming and calling.
> Calling the young and old to rest.
>   Calling the souls of those distressed,
> Longing for life everlasting.
>
> Not in our temples made with hands,
>   God, the Almighty, is dwelling.
> High in the heav'ns his temple stands,
>   All earthly temples excelling.
> Yet he who dwells in heav'ns above,
>   Deigns to abide with us in love,
> Making our bodies his temple.
>   (LBW, 365)

The words of that hymn penned by Nicolai Grundtvig in 1837 sound as though they had been written to accompany God's message to Nathan the prophet. King David had it in his mind to build a temple as a tribute to God, who instead "rains" on his plans!

> Go and tell my servant David, "Thus says the LORD: Would you build me a house to dwell in? I have not dwelt in a house since the day I brought up the people of Israel from Egypt to this day."

Do You See What I See?

God then tells Nathan to deliver those sentiments to the enthusiastic monarch who at the moment was standing ready with his "blue prints!" And the reason for the turn-down was that God saw the proposed structure more as a *cage* in which he could be *confined* than a *monument* to his *constant presence* with his people!

That, in fact, has been the insidious danger in religious buildings generally, however magnificently designed! They have tended to lull folks into believing that the space within their confines is God's real, and maybe sole, stomping grounds. They also have fed the tendencies to which you and I have a way of falling prey . . . of thinking that it is the *only* place we can look to find God! The penalty for doing that is that God seems to get lost as we go looking for him in the wrong places.

The first place many of us plant God is in *heaven*. However we envision it, it is a place far away from where we are. From the time we are taught our first prayers, we subconsciously build up mental images of God seated on a throne somewhere "out there" beyond the clouds. From that lofty perch, beyond the farthest star, he watches the workings of the earth, almost needing a telescope to see how you and I are faring.

I know that was my first understanding of God's abode as I was taught it. I can still remember my grandmother showing me a picture of Jesus, then explaining to me how he lived beyond the sun. And she used to tell me in later years how proud she was of her two-year-old grandson when he would demonstrate this knowledge for her visitors by pointing to the portrait of Christ hanging from her mantel, then lifting his hand to the sky to show where "Jesus lived."

It took a long time to get beyond those early impressions. Even now, occasionally, I catch myself thinking of God in the same way. I still lapse into the rut of thinking of him as though he is fixed somewhere in outer space. Even when I pray, rather than bow my head, I more often lift my face in the supposed direction of the one to whom I am speaking!

Or, if we don't confine God in space, we tend to coop him up in the *temple*. Even mature Christians fall prey to the idea that if there is any place on earth where God is quartered it is principally inside of this "sacred barracks." Once inside its doors,

Advent, Christmas, and Epiphany

where you *really* find God is on the *platform* where he sits in the *front of the sanctuary*. It is to that marble throne that stands there that we must turn if we want to address him face-to-face. So deeply embedded is that often-unexamined assumption in some of us that when we have a problem about which we really want to get "serious" in prayer, we feel that we must enter the seclusion of a church to be in God's presence, and to be heard.

How our orientation toward the altar as the focal point of God's presence can be read by an observer was brought home to me one summer when I was still in seminary. During Vacation Bible School, a neighboring Presbyterian church asked to bring their youngsters over to have them see how the Lutherans worshiped in their morning services. It had been requested that after the service I would take the children and their teachers on a tour of the sanctuary and explain the meaning of its symbols, and how we used them.

As I was winding up the tour, I lead the group up the chancel steps and past the choir stalls. As I tried to work my way through the crowd of youngsters, I caught an aside that nearly floored me! The tot who had appointed himself my assistant for the day blurted to his companions, as he pointed to the altar, "And *that is* the big box *where they keep Jesus.*"

Undoubtedly, our turning to and from the altar as we prayed is what planted that idea in his fertile mind. Though the altar has a different significance, and one could explain it if we had time to think about it, it had missed its mark with that young man that morning. But unless we take time to think about it, I have a sneaking suspicion that it's not just youngsters who live out the assumption that God really is boxed up in the front of the church!

A third place where we are prone to localize God is *in our own land*. It is easy to slip into the habit of tying God to our way of life and our national destiny. Without being fully aware of it at times, we can come to believe that it is only here, on *this* plot of earth, that the Almighty camps, within the boundaries of "this nation under God."

Such a tendency for people to think of themselves as God's only children is nearly as old as civilization, and as current as the past political campaign. It was powerfully present among the ancient

Do You See What I See?

Hebrews. When God told them that he had chosen them to be his people, some of them translated that to mean that they had been elevated to a pedestal from which they could look down on all other people and nations as divine cast-offs! Indeed, they were so certain that God was wrapped up solely in their dreams and destiny, that some of them believed that whoever opposed them by that fact opposed God, too!

In doing that they "wrote the book" from which many succeeding generations, including some of us, have taken leaves and lessons. More than one generation of Americans have insinuated, if not outrightly decreed, that we are the "apple" of the divine eye. With an adamant self-assurance, we have then been able to point to other lands and people and label them "outcast."

From such a pedestal we have until the very recent past written off billions of folks as "Satanic Russians" or "Godless Chinese," with clear overtones that they are rejected by God because of the political or economic systems under which they live. Even if they are members of Christian communities in those lands, they are ostracized and even picketed when they get close enough for us to let them know what status we have assigned to them from the heights of our "benevolent" position. You see, as God's elect, we can easily assume a role of semi-divinity ourselves, and set the stakes beyond which God can't be expected to be found.

The summer before last I was in East Germany again. It was a bland land, guarded by barbed wire, mine fields and soldiers armed with sub-machine guns and dogs to keep its inhabitants from leaving. Once inside you could feel the weight of such pressure to conform, where most freedoms had been wrung out of life. Most of the people we passed on the street immediately recognized us as being from the West and tried to avoid us. Even if we stopped them to ask directions, they rarely looked us in the eye. They looked over our shoulder while they answered us. Even the guide we had while there showed the same reluctance to associate with us once his duty was over. He didn't want to be accused of fraternizing with the enemy.

Just how skittish he was I learned once I arrived home. In a private moment he had given me a card with his address and asked me to send him a book of American folk songs. Soon after I was

Advent, Christmas, and Epiphany

back, I put a parcel in the mail, headed for his home. About six weeks later, a letter arrived accompanying my correspondence. It was from our guide, who wrote to tell me of his shock at receiving a communication from the States, telling me how flabbergasted he was that somehow, in a way he couldn't imagine, I had found out his address and had sent the "unwelcome item."

But that is not all there was to, or in, East Germany. I had been there before. In 1964 I was chaplain for the Thiel College Choir that toured in that country as part of its trip to the Lutheran World Federation meeting in Helsinki. And on that occasion we did more than visit churches as sorts of cultural sites and museums, as the guide showed them to us. We *sang in them with people present* . . . so many people on most evenings that even the aisles were jammed with worshipers, as many young ones as old. The music had to be submitted to the authorities beforehand. Any pieces that had any reference to the west were denied, including some of our folk songs. But some hymns of the church and the music of Bach were passed, and were permitted to be performed. What the censors let in had an effect that those of their number who were scattered in the audience wished they had had the foresight to stop.

I remember the night we sang in a church not far from the city limits of East Berlin. It was near the wall that the Russians had ordered built during one fateful night. One of the buildings on the street that was the border dividing East from West was a Lutheran church. To stop people from entering its back door, which was in the Russian zone, and exiting through the front door, which was in the American zone, and free, all the windows and doors in the front of the church were filled in with concrete blocks . . . except for two. They were tiny windows in the belfry just under the arms of a statue of Jesus stretched out in welcome. From the windows poked two machine guns ready and waiting for anyone who made a break to escape. I was chilled and filled with resentment when I looked at that building, for the land in which it stood.

That evening I was stirred and filled with another emotion. In a church so crowded that we could hardly get to our risers, we sang for more than an hour and a half to applause that nearly rocked the building. Applause, until we sang our final selection by Bach,

Do You See What I See?

based on a text from the fortieth chapter of Isaiah. It is a pasage which was written for the people who had been carried into exile by the Babylonians fifty years before:

> *Get you up to a high mountain,*
>   *O Zion, herald of good tidings;*
> *lift up your voice with strength,*
>   . . . .
> *Lift it up, be not afraid;*
>   *say to the cities of Judah,*
>   *"Behold your God!"*

When the echo died, as one person the congregation rose to its feet. There was no sound, just tears flowing from them and us as we made our way to the narthex of the church.

As I stood by the door, women stepped up to curtsey and squeeze and shake my hand. The men, usually stiff and formal, embraced me with good-byes. One of them, nearly as tall as I, reached over and pulled me close. And as he did he whispered softly to me, "We will not be afraid. God will be with us both." Before I could reply he was out the door. "Is he a pastor?" I asked one of the men who followed him out. "Him? Heavens no!" he answered. "He is a Communist who is a member of the State Ministry of Cultural Affairs."

I have thought of that man many times since. What has embedded him in my mind is that *I never had expected to hear a word like that from a member of government beyond the infamous wall.* What I had forgotten, but we all need to remember, is that this Almighty Creator of ours is a most unpredictable Lord. He refuses to be hedged in by our ideas about him. God is free to be where he chooses, and to remind us of his presence through anybody or any manner he likes! All human beings, and the whole breadth of his universe, is his arena for action.

God time and again jabs us to awaken to the fact that we can find him in the most unlikely places. Whether mountain top or cow shed, with a wooden box topped by a pair of man-made angels and carried by human porters, or in a pillar of clouds, or clothed in tongues of fire, he is apt to be there, even if the atmosphere is lacking the "aura of Holiness" we usually associate with his presence.

God is just as unfathomable in his *choice of people* through whom he will deliver his messages and help. From prophets in hair shirts to neighbors we meet raking leaves, he comes dressed in whom he chooses, when we least expect him.

You see, it's at that moment that we seem to be the farthest away from him, even perhaps when we seem to be God-forsaken, that he moves in so close that he startles us. Just when we think we have him *defined,* and therefore *confined,* he comes breaking out of our corral to sidle up to us, and pick us up, and help boost us along the way we thought we were traveling alone.

That is not to say that God is not found in places where we have come to expect him. We do feel his nearness in the moments of worship in churches like this one, in surroundings that almost reek with a sense of his closeness, in the Holy Scriptures, in the Sacraments, in the singing of liturgies, in listening to the anthems by the choirs, in the togetherness with others in the faith with whom we have walked with Jesus many times over the years. But that does not keep God from surprising us over and over again by stepping into your life and mine when we are most unaware that he is anywhere in the vicinity.

Which brings us back to David and his longing to build a house for God. For all that made sense to the King about the rightness of it all, for all the good intentions and gratitude that made that urge almost an obsession, God, with the shake of his head, sent his, "No, thank you!" to David:

> *I have not dwelt in a house since the day I brought up the people of Israel from Egypt to this day, but I have been moving about in a tent for my dwelling.*

And so it shall continue to be. No cage, however well-intentioned and beautiful, can be built big enough to satisfy God and separate this Almighty One of ours from us by fixing him at this place or other in the universe. And that means that we had better be ready constantly to have him appear from right under our noses, or maybe miss the chance of a lifetime to see him face-to-face!

The Light in the Darkness

The Nativity of Our Lord   *Isaiah 9:2-7*

Have you ever noticed how the story of Jesus' birth is set in the midst of a play of darkness and light? The whole event with its Babe and mother, the animal shed, the keepers of sheep on the hillsides, and later the Wise Men from distant places making their trek to see the Holy One, all are set alternately first in darkness then in light!

The night begins with the people of Bethlehem putting out their lamps and trudging off to bed. The city that was David's birth place goes dim, then dark, house by house. And all is at rest. Then, suddenly, a star appears, first as a mere speck, then a spot, then a fire ball punching its way through the night, pointing its finger at the stable where the peasant woman and Child are.

Shepherds are out in the fields, trying to get some rest for the night. The sheep are bedded down and the campfires that once were blazing have dwindled to glowing ashes. The flock keepers have finished swapping stories and dropped off to dreams. Then the sky lights up with a heavenly glow that brings them to their knees, blinded and frightened. A messenger of God appears and tells them the reason for the night-shattering celestial display . . . a Child has been born, and that Child is the Savior of the world. And the shepherds rush off to see for themselves the reason for it all.

Do You See What I See?

They find the stable tucked away on the hillside behind the inn. And they go in. There the darkness has been invaded by light, too! The nursery-cave is set aglow in one corner by a lamp. Under the lamp kneels a mother whose eyes shine with the light of love, made shimmering by her tears of gratitude for the safe delivery of her Baby.

And in the stone feed box lays the reason for all of the lights! The sleeping Infant! Not just another infant! But The Infant! And strangely enough, from him no light seems to come! Nowhere do we read that he shines in his cradle. There is no talk of halos. There is no supernatural glow. The lights all point to him, but do not come from him. And yet, in the retelling of the story of the night when the light exploded the darkness, it is to Jesus, not the star, not the angels, that St. John refers when he says that "the light came into the world."

Perhaps he did that because as a Jew that prophecy from the ninth chapter of Isaiah had been burned into his memory. For more than 700 years his people had waited for One to be born who would lead people out of their incessant and insane conflict with one another and with God. A "Wonderful Counsellor, Mighty God, Everlasting Father, Prince of Peace," would set foot on the earth. He would light the way to a future where "justice and righteousness" would make "trampling warriors," "battle tumult," and "garments rolled in blood" unknown.

John wrote after the Baby grew up and had lived, and died, and been resurrected. He had seen personally what the real significance of that first Christmas had been. And like all of us who have gotten beyond the surface of the event have come to learn, John saw that

> when the star had faded . . .
>
> and the gaping shepherds had died . . .
>
> and the Wise Men had gone home . . .

the One who stood as the beacon still chasing away the darkness was Jesus himself!

The Christmas story does have a lot about it that is warm and sentimental. A woman on a donkey who must give birth to a baby in a stable. Magi on camels bringing exotic gifts to pay homage. And the star! All wrap it up in mystery and excitement!

Advent, Christmas, and Epiphany

But the center of what happened is none of these. When all the external glitter and sentiment are stripped off, the light that still shines comes from the face of the One who was born . . . the one who gave the *least promise of glory* when it all began!

Yet it is he who is called "the light." Never just "a" light. Not "a light among the lights." But The Light! It is a good and proper designation for Jesus, for he has been the light of the world, showing clearer than anyone else who has ever lived, the way out of our estrangement from God and each other. If Christmas is anything, it is a festival of togetherness. It is the celebration of the coming of God to bring people back to himself and to their own kind.

Born into a world where human beings, even those related by blood, often are at each other's throats, that Baby who entered the world in a cow shed shrouded in darkness came to open our eyes to the essential oneness of the human race.

Before and after him the world has had others who have striven to show some aspects of our kinship and have worked to achieve it. But where they have tried to crack the darkness that hides us from one another by stressing that we should love one another because we are *human*, Jesus lighted up the truth that we are to love one another because we are *children of the same God*.

The difference the message of his birth made was that we should love each other not because we always are loveable, which frequently we are not! But because we are sacred beings God has seen valuable enough to come from heaven to live among. Even when our lives go sour, when we foul up ourselves and others, we are treasures that God has deemed worthy of loving, even when that act of loving is hard and expensive.

From the night when the light shined, that has been one of the truths that has separated Christianity from most other world religions. In most of them people are loved by their gods because they somehow labor to earn that love. They keep the rules of the divinity, or they make the sacrifices demanded by their holy one, or they work themselves into a lather to get in their god's good graces. In one way or another they are required to make themselves acceptable and climb into the lap of their master.

Do You See What I See?

What the Baby in the manger came to show was that all of the traveling needed to close the gap between God and people is done by God! Like himself at his birth, that gap-ending love always is a gift. It is a glowing and warming "arm-wrapping-about" event, meant even for people who have fallen flat on their faces and whose lives seem to be in constant turmoil.

The message of that Light that shone on that first Christmas is that love is like a wick burning into the wax of a candle. It creates a "well," like the palm of a hand, to gather up all sorts of folks . . . the up and rising as well as the down and outers. And in that "tub of God's love," all those who have nestled in that warming embrace are taught the miracle of how even strangers and enemies can learn to accept and find room for each other.

The miracle of Christmas is stunning in its simplicity. It is this: to end hatred and separation someone must reach out first, and take a step first, to mend spirits and tend to old wounds. The worker of that miracle should be we who have had God light up the way for us in his own earth-shattering love as it has touched our lives. He showed in Christmas that he is the One who will go to any length to take us up in his arms . . . *not wait for us to come to him* . . . where he is, for the warfare to end.

In that stable on the night the light shined, God was creating a lasting home with rooms reserved for all people. With a star lighting up the road to its door, he sent an angel choir to call all of us . . .

> *shepherds* battling with each other over pasture rights and water holes . . .
>
> > *neighbors* on your street and mine so uptight with life that they hole up in their homes and suffer in loneliness and isolation . . .
> >
> > > *Roman legionnaires* and *Jewish patriots* ready to put the whole world in flames to see whose system would rule whom . . .
> > >
> > > > and *members of families,* some perhaps sitting in churches like this one tonight, who are so ripped up by tensions and infighting with each other that they can't talk to one another, or look each other in the eyes, or touch hands anymore, even on Christmas Eve . . .

Advent, Christmas, and Epiphany

to come to him, and there to have the Light burn away the old trash, and set us aglow anew on the inside!

From that manger a Baby's cry is heard again on the night air:

> *Come here and gather tightly around my bed. When you touch each other at my manger, hold fast to those who are there, even if they are present only in your mind and heart! I have come to bring you together so that we all can be at peace!*

It is no fluffy, sentimental call that the One born this night makes urging us to help that happen. It is hard to hold on to people who have hurt you, as it is hard for them to hold on to us who have hurt them! "Peace on earth," be it between nations or between persons who live under the same roof, is tough to make a reality. Anyone who has tried to make that happen knows that. Often enormous amounts of work and pain are involved. Most "peace makers" I have known have had blistered, and sometimes bleeding, hands and hearts to show for their efforts. They have gotten them because of the perseverance and sacrifice demanded to make God's wishes for us come true.

You see, it is always *self-seeking* that leads to fracture and friction between human beings. To be at peace anywhere, in the living room, or in South Africa, or in Nicaragua, or in Bethlehem itself this very night, means that as people we must learn how to reverse ourselves. And that reversal can be excruciating because it involves *learning to live for others,* instead of *demandingly for ourselves.* It involves treating other people with the dignity and compassion we insist on for ourselves. And it forces us to take the risk of being hurt that always is possible for the ones who open themselves up first to give another a second, or fifth, or hundredth chance.

The Baby born the night the Light shined spent his entire life demonstrating and teaching how that is to be done. What he called for made some people shake their heads in astonishment and disbelief. Listen to him thirty years after the night the angels announced his arrival, and see if his formula for healing a crazy world doesn't sound off the wall:

> *"You have heard that it was said, 'You shall love your neighbor and hate your enemy.' "* (Matthew 5:43) *"But I say to you that hear, love your enemies and do good to those who hate you [Stupid!]* . . .

Do You See What I See?

> "*bless those who curse you [Ha, try that some time!]* . . .
> "*pray for those who abuse you [That will be the day!]* . . .
> "*To him who strikes you on the one cheek, offer the other also [That's the way to get your brains scrambled!]* . . .
> "*And him who takes away your cloak, do not withhold your coat as well [So you go bankrupt!]* . . .
> "*Give to everyone who begs from you [And you will soon be as poor as he is!]* . . .
> "*And of him who takes away your goods do not ask them again [financial imbecility!]* . . .
> "*And as you wish that people would do to you, do so to them [Better do it to them before they do it to you twice!]* (Luke 6:27-31)

Incredible, aren't these words? Yet, incredible as they are, these are not unapplied dictums. They are the gutsy wisdom that Jesus lived out himself before he held them up to us as an equally gutsy challenge for our living. The footer on which they all stand is this: real peace, a "locking up" and "gluing together of people" kind of peace, can only come when fists are opened up into reaching hands, when score-keeping charts on others are chucked, and when one loving, if lonely and waiting, heart rips off its barricades and opens up its doors to another.

It is frightening at times to follow this lead of Jesus: I know. I have felt it often when I tried it myself. I like to play it safe and wait for others to take such risks. But I have had people I care about die before either of us would take the first step. And at times I still grieve over what could have been but wasn't, especially on nights like this when God himself comes in the most vulnerable, risky form possible . . . a Baby, no less . . . to beg us to see in his light the way that a new start in life can be ours.

But like the birth pangs that brought that Baby to us, following his lead still can be fantastically difficult! But then, the angels who sang above his nursery did not say that peace among earthlings is ever easy. In fact, the announcement was that just the opposite is true! It will only exist among people, "with whom He is pleased." That, translated, simply means "people who will live as he has lighted the way for them to go" . . . doing those things that take some of the anger and hatred out of life in little acts that can change the heart of the world.

Advent, Christmas, and Epiphany

J. D. Salinger, in his book, *Franny and Zooey,* paints a scene in which Zooey is talking to his sister, Franny, who has been enjoying a kind of emotional breakdown. Their mother, Bessie, all aflutter with motherly concern, has been trying to get Franny to eat some of the chicken soup she has brewed to help her get back her strength. Each time Bessie comes up, cup in hand, Franny turns her down, irritated at her attempts to help.

Finally Zooey says to Franny:

> *"I'll tell you one thing, Franny . . . if it's the religious life you want, you ought to know right now that you're missing out on every single . . . religious action that is going on around this house. You don't even have enough sense to drink when somebody brings you a cup of consecrated chicken soup — which is the only kind of chicken soup Bessie ever brings to anybody around this madhouse."* (p. 196)

Ofttimes we are foolish enough to think that only giant acts, earth-shaking moves, can change the course of life. Really, it more often than not happens in small, and sometimes halting, Baby-like acts that show kindness and caring, and forgiveness and support. It is "cups of consecrated chicken soup,"
    or a hand on a shoulder . . .
        or a stammering, "Let's try again . . ."
which like a single flame that cracks even the densest gloom, truly have the power to turn heartbreak into joy!

To set that miracle of healing into motion, the Light came punching through the night! To chase the darkness that blinds us all,
    and to lighten the path to him, and meeting there, to each other,
        to show that love is the glue that he gave to hold the world together, and keep it whole . . .
God had his angels sound their trumpets, and the heavenly chorus sing. And in the stable *The Light* was born, and "the *glory* of the Lord was revealed."

Do You See What I See?

So powerful, and unchangeable, has been the Light of the Baby in the feed box that on *this* night *we sing* with Isaiah:

> *The people who walked in darkness*
>   *have seen a great light;*
> *those who dwelt in the land of the shadow of death,*
>   on them has light shined.   (Isaiah 9:2)

So be it always.

Gentle Jesus

Christmas 1   *Isaiah 45:22-25*

Gentle Jesus, Meek and Mild
Look upon a little child.
Christian children all must be
Mild, obedient, good as He.

So the opening lines of a children's hymn sketch the portrait of Jesus Christ and his friends. Wielding a brush that draws with colors we all recognize, it traces a picture of Christ that is so widely accepted among us that it is seldom, if ever, viewed with a critical eye.

It is especially true of the portraits of him that fill this season of the year. He is always the cuddly infant, resting on his mother's lap, and she with a far-away look in her eye, surrounded by just-washed cattle in a stable so clean you could eat off its floor. It is so comforting a view of the new-born King that we are lulled into thinking that he *remained a cooing infant* for the rest of his earthly stay, never growing up, never gathering the disciples, never having to face the challenges of the mission he was born to carry out . . . and most certainly never becoming One who would demand anything from anybody or ever utter the word "No!"

Do You See What I See?

Yes, from the manger to the grave, and beyond, whether it is Raphael or Sallman, our image-makers have tended to envision Jesus as a quiet, mild-mannered person with an almost effeminate aspect. The Baby born in Bethlehem will walk through life patting babes on the head, posing with lambs in his arms and blessing everyone, tactfully choosing his steps and his words. The last thing the One whose birth the angels announced will do is grow up and offend anyone with what he does or says.

It is these portraits that contribute to the jolt we get when we run up against the words God speaks through Isaiah:

> "I am God, and there is no other.
> By myself I have sworn,
> from my mouth has gone forth in
> righteousness
> a work that shall not return:
> 'To me every knee shall bow,
> every tongue shall swear.'
> "Only in the LORD, it shall be said
> of me, are
> righteousness and strength;
> to him shall come and be ashamed,
> all who were incensed against him.
> In the LORD all the offspring of
> Israel
> shall triumph and glory . . ."

The strength of these words can send chills up our backs! If they are to be applied to the One whose birth angels announced, it is not the cooing infant of our imagination that we are dealing with in the Divine One, but a **Lord,** a **Master,** to whom "all who were incensed against him" will one day get on their knees and "be ashamed." Even though we are just a week away from the scene of the Infant in the stables, the lessons for this day want us to remember who that Baby was . . . and what his coming was to mean for the lives of those who follow him . . . and for those who refuse!

When we meet him in the New Testament, that fact is made clear. For there, more often than the casual reader might often

Advent, Christmas, and Epiphany

suspect, his words are shot through with tones of sharpness and challenge, and sometimes even of threat:

> *"Not everyone who says to me, Lord, Lord shall enter the kingdom of heaven, but he that does the will of my Father . . . ."* (Matthew 7:21)

> *"For I tell you, unless your righteousness exceeds that of the Scribes and Pharisees, you will* never *enter the kingdom of heaven."* (Matthew 5:20)

And when he says things like that, the Baby-become-Man surprises us because he seems to be stepping out of character. Instead of being in his mother's lap, or having a lamb in his arms, he walks through the world with his finger tapping individuals on the chest demanding something from them. And making **demands** is not what we associate with "Gentle Jesus, meek and mild" . . . nor with the Christian faith, for the most part. Harry F. Baughman put it this way:

> *"Somehow, we feel that whatever exactions life . . . may make of us, it is the special function of [our Lord and] our religion to provide relief and make us comfortable. Jesus our Master whom we serve is compassionate, tender and forgiving . . . . He of all with whom we may have to do . . . is not exacting."*
> (Gettysburg Lutheran Seminary Bulletin, 1957)

Science is demanding of its practitioners; that we know. Unless you follow a formula precisely and work the mathematics out to pinpoint accuracy, your experiment is apt to fail — or you may even get your head blown off!

Business is exacting, too, isn't it? Make repeated mistakes in judgment or performance, and you are apt to end up not only with holes in your shoes, but bankruptcy lawyers on your back.

But when we come to our *religion* and *its practice,* and its *Christ,* we expect something else again. Here we want a lot of leeway and wide tolerances with which to work. We're sure that if we fail in our religious commitments, God will wink at it. Should we be lax in carrying out his will for us today . . . well, there will always be tomorrow. Our God is a God of love, and that is translated to mean that we can rest assured that he will write off all of our slip-shod antics as human frailty. For as Omar Khayyam said of the Christian's God, "He's a good fellow and 'twill all be well."

And so it is with a shudder that we ponder that passage from Isaiah:

> "I am God, and there is no other.
>   By myself I have sworn,
>   from my mouth has gone forth in
>   righteousness
>   a work that shall not return:
> 'To me every knee shall bow,
>   every tongue shall swear.'
> "Only in the LORD, it shall be said
>   of me, are
>   righteousness and strength;
> to him shall come and be ashamed,
>   all who were incensed against him."

And it keeps shaking us when Jesus lays his axe to the root of that religious tree with those words of his:

> "Not everyone who says to me Lord, Lord, shall enter the kingdom of heaven . . . . Unless your righteousness exceeds that of the scribes and Pharisees you *shall never enter the kingdom* . . . ."

They fall on us like a ton of bricks. For what is done in those two devastating strokes is that the easy sentimental idea that religion is more thought than action, and that piety consists of kindly phrases without hard, consecrated work are ripped out!

Words like these have always been a blast to those who took them to heart. Isaiah's own contemporaries thought of God, too, as a soft-headed Santa Claus type who constantly handed out but never held people accountable for their lives and actions. All that was necessary to stay on good terms with him was *pray* once in a while, perhaps *go to the temple* occasionally, say you were *sorry* periodically for the sins you committed but loved so much you intended to go right on doing. That together should supply a package that would keep the Old Boy contented.

Advent, Christmas, and Epiphany

Their easy-going idea about religion was so persuasive that the prophet Hosea portrayed one Israelite saying flippantly to another:

> *"Come let us return to the Lord for He hath torn, and he will heal us. After two days He will restore us. In the third day He will raise us up."*

That's how easy it was, or how easy people liked to think it was. That's still how easy people like to think it is to be a child of God. "God doesn't demand much," they've convinced themselves. Just get to church when it is not inconvenient, pray when it moves you, especially when we get in a bind. Give God a few fleeting thoughts, when we can spare them, and we've done all that can be expected. After all, "He's a good fellow and 'twill all be well!"

Look around and check it out. See if this is so or not. The evidence pops up everywhere that religion is a side-line affair in life to be relied upon when we are over-the-barrel. Droves of people only come to God like puppies romping to their feed-bowl. Then they romp off to regions unknown once their bellies are full.

For files-full of individuals the church is a community that fulfills their needs at times of *hatchin'*, *matchin'* and *dispatchin'*. Faces you never see at other times appear when babies are born — reappear when a wedding chapel is needed — and then again when a funeral must be faced. In between they hide in the weeds — except when pain or tragedy strikes.

If God had a nickel for every person who swore he or she would cling to him like glue if he pulled them through a crisis, then deserted him as soon as they were on their feet, the funds would be available to feed every needy person of the world everyday of the year.

Almost weekly calls come to us from people who are in a bind, and who for the moment claim our parish as their church, but who for decades have never darkened its doors . . . or identified themselves with its mission in the name of Jesus Christ. It is so nearly everywhere. And what people do with the *church* is usually a shadow of where *God fits* into their existence. He is a "last straw" to reach for in extreme times.

Thirty years ago there were heady discussions going on in philosophical circles about whether God had died or not. By and large, few individuals ever get involved with go-arounds like that. But we all are up to our ears in the practical, earthy, day-to-day struggle with *that issue.* Is God *alive* for you? . . . and how and where and how vitally is he wrapped up in what you say and do?

Too many want to keep God at arm's length. They want to set their own moral codes. They want God to keep his nose out of their checkbooks, or personal relationships, or out of parked cars, or from behind locked doors. If he is *alive* for them, they want to keep him *tranquilized* so that he doesn't get in the way.

And if he does, and they get caught in a bind, then they try another ace they have up their sleeves. All they have to do to be home free after they have had their fling is to tell God that they will *repent.* That word, you see, ought to smooth out that weepy-One in the heavens and see that all we piled up in our debit ledger is cancelled out!

What such popular religion does is misunderstand what repentance means as the Bible teaches it. To *repent* means to be so sorry for what you have done that you stop doing it! In the New Testament *metanoia* means to have your whole mind do a revolution so that all of your thinking has been turned over. In the Old Testament the word *shuv* means to turn around and walk in the opposite direction from the one in which you are moving. Both would leave behind that which was wrong and head in God's direction. Saying you are sorry for what you have done, but that you love it too much to give it up, is not repentance. In a biblical sense that is *blaspheming* because what it really involves is telling God that *you* are your *Lord* . . . not *him.*

Doing that, repeatedly, is one of the most dangerous games we play in life. It leads to a pattern of self-deception that is difficult to break. Repeatedly pushing God away when he moves into our lives develops a resistance that we can take with us to the grave. Like cement, we can so harden ourselves that even God can find it impossible to break through. That is why I am convinced that very few people are saved on their death beds. When a determined resister faces death, what they often feel is *fear* — not faith. With what, for them, is the unknown looming before them, often they panic from a life of emptiness. And the Bible does not say "by *fear* you are saved," but by *faith* and the *grace* of God.

Advent, Christmas, and Epiphany

Long before that moment arrives for any of us, God is at work trying to link up with us. He keeps *calling* and *reaching* and *pushing* and at times *threatening* us to get our attention and make us his. To be his disciples is not simply a matter of mouthing occasional pious sentiments. It involves *obedience,* the living out of the love that we have for him if he is our Lord in fact.

One day, while Jesus was traveling through Galilee, a young ruler came running up to meet him on the road. Falling at Jesus' feet, the rich youth told Jesus of his desires to find eternal life. He went on to tell the Carpenter what he already had done to prepare himself for it.

In every way he seemed to be admirably well-qualified to obtain what he had come seeking. Morally, he had most of his life in line and his eyes fixed on the commendable goal. He had even come to Jesus in a spirit of humility. Rather than stand, he had kneeled before him in the dusty road.

Yet, in the face of all that seemed so outstanding and praiseworthy, Jesus focused his attention on a *weakness* in the lad. "One thing you still lack . . . Go, sell all that you have, and come follow me." In the presence of an already *high* degree of moral excellence, Jesus chose to talk about the one item of debit.

It was Jesus' way of showing just how demanding and exacting he really is to those who are his. He won't settle for minimums. He wants controlling interest in our lives. The Pharisees, whom he told his disciples they had to excel, were the outstanding people of their community. They fasted twice each week to show their piety. They gave ten percent of all that they had to support the work of God. They did not stay in the "sack" when the services were going on at the Temple or Synagogue. And still, what Jesus demanded of his own followers was *more*, not *less* than *that!*

What he wanted was *righteousness* in the sense in which Isaiah uses it in the Old Testament Lesson for today. The word means to give one what is due him or her because of the claim they have on your life. If God is the Master, the Lord, the Supreme One, then he is the One who deserves to be in command and set the pattern for all that we do and are. The crucial fact of the Christian faith is that that is the role which Jesus demands in every one of our lives.

Do You See What I See?

This does not mean that we earn God's love, or buy our salvation, by our obedience. As evangelical Christians we hold fast to the truth that "By grace you are saved through faith," as St. Paul declared. "By grace" means that nothing you or I can do in any way merits eternity for us. We can't deserve it because of our acts. We can't bargain for it in any way. God gives it to us freely, out of his loving heart. And we have to accept it on those terms by trusting that proffer by faith.

But that only deepens the claim that God has on our lives and loyalties. As St. Paul also reminds us:

> *When you were slaves to sin you were free in regards to righteousness.... But now ... you have been set free from sin and have become slaves of God.* (Romans 6:20)

Slaves of God! Owned, bought and paid for by him for no other reason than that he loved us. Now that we are his, he doesn't release us from our obedience to him. In fact, he expects more from us than from those who write him off.

Moses made the point with the people of Israel that God had set free from Egypt. After God had saved them from Pharaoh, as a gift, he had Moses give them the facts of their new life:

> *See, I have set before you this day life and good, death and evil. If you obey the Commandments of the Lord your God which I command you this day, by loving the Lord your God, by walking in his ways and keeping his Commandments ... then you shall live and multiply, and the Lord your God will bless you in the land which you are entering.... But if your heart turns away, and you will not hear, but are drawn away to worship other gods and serve them, I declare this day, that you shall perish.*
> (Deuteronomy 30:15-18)

Jesus put an exclamation point after that when he began his ministry, reminding his hearers that obedient and committed hearts had not passed out with the Patriarchs. Faith that produced lives shaped by his will was still par for the course for the people of God.

St. John tells us that, when Jesus began to lay that on the line, droves of hangers-on began to leave his side. "This is a hard

Advent, Christmas, and Epiphany

saying," they grumbled. "Who can listen to it?" they muttered as they walked away. And so many followed that Jesus turned to the twelve and asked them, "Will you also go away?" (John 6:60, 67) It was Simon Peter who answered for them all, as usual. "Lord to whom shall we go? You have the words of eternal life and we have believed." (John 6:68-69)

The days and years that followed, while often trying ones for those who held fast to him, proved Peter to be right. The demanding Jesus, to whom they bowed as Lord, they learned to see was the Gentle Jesus who never abandoned them along the way. Along with his demands came the strengthening hand that held the lives together of those who stayed with him and put their destinies in his hand.

And that still is the way it is today! The demands that God makes on us have always had a single purpose: to press us to let him, who knows what life really is like, and where its numerous paths lead, guide us with his strong, sure hands through its pitfalls and temptations to eternal wholeness . . . and home. For his is the only hand that has the power to lead us into that abiding Kingdom.

Getting Out of Your Own Way

Christmas 2   *Isaiah 61:10—62:3*

About a dozen years ago I took up the sport of trapshooting. I got into it as a diversion to get me away from total involvement with work, and because I liked guns but had gotten tired of killing things.

It is a sport in which a shotgun is used to break clay targets called pigeons, which really are shaped like saucers rather than birds! They are thrown by machines called traps, which launch them into the air at about seventy-five miles an hour. The idea is to shatter them before they can hit the ground.

When you stand and watch the targets being thrown, they look as big as pies. You would wonder how anyone could miss one of the things. The fact is that those pigeons fly as if equipped with radar! They seem to duck in and out of the pellets you shoot at them as if they were alive!

Usually you test your skill by shooting at twenty-five targets in succession. With four other persons in a squad, you fire to break as many as possible. A complete round of trap is four events of twenty-five birds each. At the end of 100 targets, the person who has hit the most is the winner. If two are tied, they must keep shooting until one scores higher than the other.

Do You See What I See?

Such tie-breakers are called "shoot offs." Each person picks up a new box of shells and goes back into competition to win. If both are still tied when those twenty-five shots have been fired, they do it all over again until one misses at least one target more than the other.

Well, I had a hard time of it when I got started in the sport. Out of twenty-five targets I was lucky to break eight or nine. I remember excitedly calling home to tell my wife the news the day I broke fifteen out of twenty-five! But, eventually, I got the hang of how it was done, and things improved.

Three months later I entered an event involving several hundred shooters. After two days, and 500 targets, another man and I were tied for the lead. The other fellow was a veteran of the sport, with a name well-known in trapshooting circles. When the time came to shoot against this fellow whom I had read about in magazines, my heart was in my mouth!

We got our shells and took our places in front of the grandstands filled with spectators. We started firing away, and at the end of twenty-five targets we each had broken them all. Twice more we went at it, and at the end of seventy-five, neither one of us had lost a bird. It was then that we had to go to buy another box of shells to try to settle things.

When I got back to my position, the other shooter was nowhere in sight. Finally he appeared, carrying in his arms a twenty-box case of shells. I stood there with my mouth open as he calmly ripped open the carton, and piled the boxes up on the walk behind him. Then, turning to me, he walked up and said, "I don't know about you, but I don't plan to miss another target today. You might just as well get that through your head right now!"

He picked up his gun and called for his target and smashed it to smithereens! I called for mine, and missed it by a yard! Twenty-four birds later it was all over. He walked off of the field with the winner's trophy under his arm.

As I headed past the stands with my chin on my chest, an old gentleman whom I had never met leaned out of the bleachers as I went by, "Don't take it so hard, young fellow. There will be another day. You could be standing where he is right now. All you have to do is learn *how to get out of your own way!*"

Advent, Christmas, and Epiphany

It took me a while to understand what that fellow meant. I was in my car on my way home when it finally sank in. What had beaten me that day in the shoot-off was not my lack of ability to break targets. It was my self-doubt and anxiety which that veteran had aroused in me that made me beat myself! I had lost that match because I had convinced myself that I couldn't keep up doing what I already had been doing all afternoon. I doubted that I had the potential to achieve the goal I longed for. The moment that doubt took over, I was whipped. I talked myself into defeat as certain as can be.

That experience underlines something that you and I do repeatedly in life. *We are constantly getting into our own way and setting ourselves up for failure.* We muff chance after chance and fail to make our dreams a reality because we convince ourselves that we can't!

The most frequent cause for such lost opportunities is that inner voice that keeps whispering, "You are going to lose! You are sure to louse it up! That challenge is too big for you!" And we believe that voice. And, in believing, we prepare to trip ourselves up. We end up falling flat on our faces, not because of the hurdles thrown up from the *outside,* but from the *ones built on the inside* by our own *attitudes.*

That is why Shapespeare hits the nail on the head when he has Cassius speak for us all as he says to his friend: "The fault, dear Brutus, is not in our stars but in ourselves that we are underlings." (*Julius Caesar,* Act 1, Scene 2)

The Israelites who had been carted off into exile would have understood our situation. They had become convinced that they were losers of the first rank, too. And it was not clay targets that they had dropped that had put them in the doldrums. Their farms and businesses had been wiped out, their nation pillaged, and some of their family members killed, or separated from them, by the Babylonian army that had conquered, then utterly humiliated, them. Even when, a generation later, the Persians had done in the Babylonians and offered the Hebrews the chance to return home and start rebuilding, most of them shook their heads "No" and hunkered down to stay put in Babylon. What would be the use of a long trek back to a country in ruins? If they did make it back, they wouldn't have the stuff needed to get it all back together anyway! And if they did get something started, what was the use of working your head off only to have another marauding army come in and knock it all off into a heap again? Nothing really changes. Life is the pits. It's the same old turn of events served up in another recipe time after time!

Jesus also understood our plight when he dealt with the throngs of people who came to him with sagging and frazzled lives. When they turned to him for ways of dealing with their existence in new and productive ways, he gave them the secrets that could and can unlock them from their miseries. The key to making the most of our opportunity is to be found in the word "confidence." That is why one of Jesus' frequent questions and challenges to the folks who pressed in around him was wrapped up in the powerful word, "Believe."

When a pair of men pleaded for his healing as he entered Jericho, his first response to them was, "Do you believe I can do this?" And when his disciples saw Jesus' power to bring their concrete problems of existence to heel, and longed to have it for themselves, he turned their eyes toward the most staggering obstacles they could imagine and challenged them to have confidence as well: "Truly I say to you, if you have faith as a grain of mustard seed . . . nothing shall be impossible for you." (Matthew 17:20b, 21b)

What Jesus said was not meant for an elite few. It was a promise he made to us all. For God has gifted us with enormous potential to achieve and develop as persons. And he wants us to tap those gifts for others' and our own good, as well. He means for all of us to be what we secretly long to become and reach those plains in living which we bury for the most part because we are afraid to then make public lest we be laughed at for even imagining!

To get us into action, he jabs and urges us to trust the promises he made: that you and I have what it takes, when we feel down and out, to get up and take charge of our lives and shape them and the world in stunning and beautiful ways. We have been given what it takes to be "winners," wherever winning needs to be done in our lives. The ingredient needed to get us up and out of our own ways is the faith to open the door for God to let his power flow into us and juice us up for the challenge at hand! That is why Jesus urges us:

> *"Ask and it shall be given to you . . .*
> *Seek and you will find . . .*
> *Knock and it will be opened to you . . . ."*

Until we *ask* and *seek* and *know,* that is until we act on his promise to be ready to help us, nothing ever will change in dramatic ways. Chief among the chains that keeps us from doing any of these things is the almost universal "lock" of a low self image.

And God, through Isaiah, was trying to pick that "lock" in laying out the assurance and challenge we hear read in the promises of the Old Testament Lesson for today:

> *"I will greatly rejoice in the LORD,*
>   *my soul shall exult in my God;*
> *for he has clothed me with the*
>   *garments of salvation,*
> *he has covered me with the robe of*
>   *righteousness,*
> *as a bridegroom decks himself with a*
>   *garland,*
> *and as a bride adorns herself with*
>   *her jewels.*
> *For as the earth brings forth its*
>   *shoots,*
> *and as a garden causes what is sown*
>   *in it to spring up,*
> *so the Lord GOD will cause*
>   *righteousness and praise*
> *to spring forth before all the nations.*
>   *for Zion's sake I will not keep silent,*
> *and for Jerusalem's sake I will not*
>   *rest,*
> *until her vindication goes forth as*
>   *brightness,*
> *and her salvation as a burning torch.*
>   *The nations shall see your vindication,*
>   *and all the kings your glory;*
> *and you shall be called by a new name*
>   *which the mouth of the LORD will*
>   *give.*

Do You See What I See?

> *You shall be a crown of beauty in the*
> *hand of the LORD,*
> *and a royal diadem in the hand of*
> *your God."*

Unfortunately, much of its push for hope in a new tomorrow, that we will see, is lost because we put the words in an "other worldly" frame of reference every time we hear them! The roadblock in the passage is that word "salvation." It is a term we usually think comes into action once death closes our eyes. It has to do with life after this earthly stay. It is heaven-bound. But the fact of the matter is that the word in Hebrew does not usually refer to what happens after we die at all. The original term is *yasha*. It literally means "to push back the walls." It has in mind the act of shoving out of the way whatever it is that threatens to hem us in, or cut us off from living. It, therefore, has to do with opening up new ways to be free to live out the next possibility that is headed our way, with getting freed from whatever it is that paints us into a corner, or cuts us off from getting on positively and passionately with our lives. Only after that is understood does *yasha* have to do with a next life that will come when this one has run its course.

Understood in this sense, you can see what good news Isaiah has to deliver to folks who get hemmed in and locked up by the negatives that bombard them. Built most often from a steady stream of words that fall like axes on the root of a tree, we get taught early that we are losers, destined for mediocrity. A barrage of "downers" drop on us like rain informing us:

"You can't do that!"

"You'll never get it right!"

"Put that dream out of your head!"

And these "word-bombs" usually are lobbed at us by people who themselves have had the same nets thrown over them in the past. Having their confidence drained away, they warn us about the "practicalities of life." They advise us:

"It is better to be safe than sorry."

"Only fools rush in where angels fear to tread."

"What will be will be!"

The summary of it all is that what others have found to be awesome and difficult is surmountable for us, too!

Advent, Christmas, and Epiphany

The sad thing about even such well-meaning crepe hangers is that they sow the seeds that produce the destructive thoughts that call God a liar when he builds into us visions of what he has designed us to be and do. It breeds "rats of doubt" that gnaw away at the pulley of faith and often brings it down. It keeps hanging out the sign "Impossible" on the visions God gives to each one of us.

This goes on even though psychiatrists tell us that no human being ever uses more than ten to twenty percent of his or her potential mind power. Even that level can be triggered only when a challenge is perceived and accepted! It is then that we forget our limits and astonishing things occur.

I remember seeing a mother, whose family lived on our street, run to her son who had just been hit by a truck loaded with slabs of marble. Its rear wheels were resting on his arm. Although she weighed no more than 110 pounds, and was only a little over five feet tall, I gasped with the others as we watched her pick up the back of that truck and move it off of her child!

We know how scientists stood in awe, and patients poured out their thanks, when, after thousands of years of pain, an undeterred researcher produced the substance that escaped all others, and gave us ether to make surgery a God-send for healing!

The world is blessed with people in every walk of life who have refused to give up just because others had thrown in the towel. They did the seemingly impossible because they had turned loose the inner power that was theirs. They are like that magnificent creature whose praises were written out on a plaque my home room teacher had hanging over her desk:

> *The Bumble Bee is an aeronautical disaster. Its body is too heavy for its wing area and it is drastically underpowered. Its center of gravity is too far to the rear for it to be air worthy. Thus his ability to launch is lost . . . But the Bumble Bee does not know this — so he flies!*

What the bee, like its human counterparts, can do is try with all that is in it to reach for the outer limits. What can keep us grounded is the refusal to *believe that we can,* when we have the chance to launch for the stars.

Do You See What I See?

What I have learned is this . . . the only time *things* really are *impossible,* and life's puzzles unsolvable, is when we *believe* that they are. For what we believe is real often becomes so. If we believe what others call "impossible" really isn't, virtual miracles can begin to happen in our lives.

That word "miracle" in the New Testament is the Greek term *dunamis.* It has come into our tongue as "dynamite!" It refers to powerful things that come into being when God blows away the obstacles to his will being done in nature or in history — *world* history or *personal* histories.

It also describes the absolutely mind-bending event that can occur when God succeeds in getting you and me to light the fuse to the potential he breathed into us with the breath of life! An "explosive" is already hidden in us, as a divine gift! To set it off, we must get out of the way so the divine "match" can touch the fuse. If we do . . . look out! The results can be spectacular!

The second thing that keeps us getting in our own way is the *fear of success!* It is an affliction that infects many people most of the time, and all of us some of the time. We fear succeeding because once we do it, then the expectation arises for us to do it again, and again! If you and I show that we can win and achieve in any area of life, then we lose the safety that being perpetual failures gives. If we never seem to be able to do anything worthwhile, no one, including ourselves, can expect anything from us. And we can relax, and stay securely in our ruts. You see, getting out of the old cocoon, while it is surrounded with a whole new freedom and its set of possibilities, can be scary since we don't know what demands may come with them!

The Hebrews experienced that when God acted on their pleas to free them from slavery in Egypt. Into the mud pits he sent a deliverer, Moses, and through him took the Israelites by the hand to lead them into a Promised Land, where their lives were theirs to live as they chose. And as they moved out of their slave cabins after the Passover was ended, they were jubilant at leaving their chains and taskmasters behind.

But hardly had they gotten out of sight of the Egyptians when they began to have second thoughts! As free people, they had to feed themselves. Without overseers, they had to learn how to

Advent, Christmas, and Epiphany

organize as a family so that each of them could live without destroying the other. With hostile nations surrounding them, they had to arm themselves and battle for their own defense. And there in the desert, with all these problems, while they were on their way to the Land of their dreams, they began to long for the "good old days" . . . when as the property of Pharaoh they had been secure and provided for!

In Egypt they had known where their next meal was coming from. It was not a banquet, mind you, but it was *assured!* And *jobs* were theirs to work at. It was making bricks and carrying mortar, but at least there was no unemployment! And others took care of the threats from without! They were not free to launch out on their own. But as owned people, no one had to take the risk and danger that were built into freedom. So, like an eternal adolescent complaining about the restrictions and demands of the parent, but loving the predictability of the familiar, they grumbled with Moses and began to yearn for the security of their chains again!

That love of the safety and predictability of being among the "unable" keeps us standing in our own way at one juncture after another. The temptation is to tie ourselves to an anchor, refusing to budge or try out our potential. Because, you see, to launch out always involves the fear of risk, just as its possibilities are thrilling!

I have been reading about eagles lately. These magnificent birds build nests where the eggs they lay, and the young that they hatch, sit high in trees or on rock ledges that hang out over canyon walls, often at dizzying heights! Once the young eaglets are born, they sit in the nest and are fed and coddled by the parents who work tirelessly to fill their every need.

As the fledglings grow, their down is replaced by feathers and soon they begin to flap their wings, rising above the nest. But they do not fly! They drop back into the nest and wait to be fed and protected by the adults. Their wings seem to be only toys with which they entertain themselves and each other. Left to themselves they would grow into adults and never do anything more than flop above the nest and fall back into its protection once again.

But when they show sufficient potential to hover over the nest, the parents begin to edge them toward its sides. First they coax them with food. Then they push them with their heads. They keep

Do You See What I See?

moving them out until the eaglets are perched on the edge of the nest, clutching it with their talons. They will not let go! They want to go back into the center of the nest! But the struggle goes on, until, with a mighty push, the adults shove the eaglets out into space! Even though they are eagles, they must be taught to let go and reach. Only then are they enabled to climb to the heights they were built and destined to attain!

People, too, must be taught to soar and use our powers to attain the heights we were built and destined for. God read us that birthright when he told us to: "Be fruitful and multiply and fill the earth and subdue it and have dominion . . . ."(Genesis 1:28) It is vital for us to remember that in order for us to soar to the heights that God shows each of us in our "heart's desire," we must let go of the "nests," whatever they look like in our individual lives, and let God launch us. We have to get out of our own way, and stop being our own worst enemies. We must trust God's promise that we can rise out of the death of the old ways and the old binds — and trust the way God shows us to be open!

Unless we do that, as scary as it can be to take the chance of falling on our faces as we learn to succeed and soar, of stumbling the first, tenth, or hundredth time, we will never know the exhilaration of really breathing free!

God built the desire to achieve into all of us. When we cheer Rocky Balboa, in I, II, III, IV or whatever number it will be next, rising from stumble bum to champ, or see a handicapped individual succeed at a venture in life that had been labeled "unthinkable," or personally dream about whatever it is that we see in our hearts in our secret moments . . . we are uged by God to flap those divinely given wings and launch out.

And God, that Divine Nagger of ours, will never let us sit in safety in peace! He will keep conjuring up new possibilities, fanning the desire to be, telling us to get out of our own way and trust him to help us leave the rut of our own way and trust him to help us reach for the vision that is in our hearts. Then:

> ". . . you *shall be called by* a new name
> which the mouth of the LORD will
> give.
> You shall be a crown of beauty *in the*
> hand of the LORD,
> and a royal diadem in the hand of
> your God."

Thank You, God, for Wanting Me!

The Baptism of Our Lord   Isaiah 42:1-7

"**Too** soon old, too late smart," is the way the old Dutch proverb says it. From my experience, at least, what it says is right on the button in describing our plight. It does seem to take much of a lifetime to learn some of the most crucial lessons of existence. And it is just as true that we often get the point when it is too late to do anything about it, or nearly so.

Haven't you said, as I have, "If only I knew *then* what I know *now*," or, "Oh, if I only had it to do all over again"? Our longing is to grab the hands of life's clock and turn them back, while holding on to what we have learned as they were spinning forward. That is why, in the rock opera, *Jesus Christ Super Star*, Peter is speaking for all of us when he pleads with Jesus:

> This was unexpected, what do I do now?
> Hurry up and tell me this is just a dream!
> Could we start again, please? Could we start again?

The crusher, of course, is that time runs only in one direction. The TV commercial, sad to say, is right on target for this world, at least, when it tells us, "You only go around once."

Do You See What I See?

That being so, sometimes God gives us a gift that is nearly as effective as turning back time. It is the gift of revelation and sensitivity, which in combination can help us wake up before it is too late to catch hold of this or that corner of life and turn it in a new direction while we still have the time and opportunity. When that happens, one has the chance "to get smart" before "it is too late!"

During the last few years of my life, God has given me such an opportunity. My whole life has been turned in new directions, and my eyes have been opened to see life with a depth that was largely hidden from me before. Maybe it has come as a result of the jolt of having our children grow up and leave home, forcing me to look at them and our home and the future differently, and with more reflection. Perhaps it has happened because I have been engaged intensely with people who have had to struggle with brutal, life-threatening experiences, and have had to watch them end up shredded or dead. Or maybe I have been opened up and softened as I have sat with people who have had the bottoms drop out of their lives as marriages have crumbled, or have had their kids ravaged by drugs. In instance after instance, life has looked like a nightmare, a kind of waterslide heading downward to a yawning whirlpool.

The effect of it all has been to push me to sift through life, theirs and mine, to try to find what it is that really matters. Where is there hope for a good tomorrow? And, in the searching, I have reexperienced the bedrock human longing to be a whole and truly fulfilled human being. I have learned that for that to be realized there are four things that we must have:

1. A sense of belonging to someone, somewhere.
2. A sense of personal worth and value.
3. A sense of security, an anchor to which we can tether our lives when everything else seems to be coming loose.
4. A sense of purpose, a star by which we can set the course of our lives, and a cause to which we can give ourselves that will give us a reason for living and make existence complete and worthwhile.

These needs, these human hungers, exist in every human being regardless of our role or position in life, or wherever and whenever we live. For so many people I meet, these needs and longings go unfulfilled most of the time. There are endless lines of folks who appear hopeless, who surrounded by material plenty are starving to death inside, who outwardly are successful but within are empty and continually dissatisfied, who live in crowds and are surrounded by people, but who feel adrift and alone. What makes life so miserable is that they think they have nowhere to turn or go to have their hunger satisfied.

I am convinced that, of all the places on earth, those needs can only be fully met in the presence and arms of Jesus Christ, and in the company of his earthly family we call the church. As I see it, the purpose at the very heart of our life together as God's people is to act as God's agents in trying to fill each of these longings in one another; and to carry that message to God's people, to whom he will bless us with the opportunities to do just that! If you and I are willing to let God use us, and let him be our Guide and Provider, we can make a magnificent difference in our families, in our circles of friends, in our places of business and in the midst of the communities where we live. And in that process of serving, our own lives, along with those of the ones who will be drawn into our fellowship, will be filled full and given a vibrancy we may find astonishing.

About 2,600 years ago, speaking to a group of Israelites in a far-off land to which they had been carted away as prisoners when their nation had been conquered and destroyed, the prophet Isaiah saw God as providing the light that gave hope to people who were in tatters. For nearly three generations they had been forced to stay in a land which most of them despised. Longing to go home, they grieved that tomorrow would be as hopeless and as dark and as empty as yesterday. One of them, putting his despair into words, cried out:

> *By the waters of Babylon*
> *there we sat down and wept, when*
> *we remembered Zion.*
> *On the willows there we*
> *hung up our lyres*

Do You See What I See?

> *For there our captors required of us songs*
> *and our tormentors mirth, saying,*
> *"Sing us one of the songs of Zion."*
> *How shall we sing the Lord's song in a strange land?*
> (Psalm 137:1-3)

It was into that kind of gloom that Isaiah, at a later date, reaching up for that harp that had been hung in the tree in despair, played a new and different tune, the words of which appear in our Old Testament Lesson for today:

> *"Behold my servant, whom I uphold,*
> *my chosen, in whom my soul*
> *delights;*
> *I have put my Spirit upon him,*
> *he will bring forth justice to the*
> *nations.*
> *He will not cry or lift up his voice,*
> *or make it heard in the street;*
> *a bruised reed he will not break,*
> *and a dimly burning wick he will not*
> *quench;*
> *he will faithfully bring forth justice.*
> *He will not fail or be discouraged*
> *till he has established justice in the*
> *earth;*
> *and the coastlands wait for his law.*
> *Thus says God, the LORD,*
> *who created the heavens and*
> *stretched them out,*
> *who spread forth the earth and what*
> *comes from it,*
> *who gives breath to the people upon it*
> *and spirit to those who walk in it:*
> *"I am the LORD, I have called you in*
> *righteousness,*
> *I have taken you by the hand and*
> *kept you;*
> *I have given you as a covenant to the*
> *people, a light to the nations,*
> *to open the eyes that are blind,*
> *to bring out the prisoners from the*
> *dungeon,*
> *from the prison those who sit in*
> *darkness."*

Advent, Christmas, and Epiphany

These words of God have had at least two frames of reference embedded in them over the ages. One, of course, has been seen by the Christian church to be a prophecy concerning the coming of Christ, who would be "[God's] chosen in whom [His] soul delights," the One God had, "put [His] Spirit upon," and who would, "bring forth justice to the nations." But they also were understood to have a second dimension, or "level," of prophecy about them. They were understood to be a description of the "people of God," both Israel and the church, who were called to be agents of God to get that very task accomplished! When the Lord said through Isaiah:

> "I am the LORD, I have called you in
>   righteousness,
> I have taken you by the hand and
>   kept you;
> I have given you as a covenant to the
>   people, a light to the nations . . . ."

it was to us that the eye-opening call of God to get up and to get going to help get that task accomplished was being given, too! God was there, on the spot, to link up with them (and us), and make their hopelessness evaporate. Through them the Lord was going to reach out to others who were at loose ends to let them know that they were indeed his people as well, with no "ifs" or "ands" about it!

That realization that *we really belong to Someone,* with a small "s" as well as a large one, somewhere, is one of the central needs of every person. So strong is it that I believe it runs a close third after food and water as a necessity of life. It is so crucial that we will trade almost anything to get it. I have watched when, in despair and panic, people have sold or given away their possessions, their bodies, their integrity, even life itself, just to hear someone say, "I love you."

One of the tragic realities in too many lives is that that assurance is never experienced. Whether missed, or never present, some folks go through life feeling cut off, left out, unwanted and achingly

Do You See What I See?

alone. For millions of them the haunting strains of that old spiritual catches up and underlines their pain:

> *Sometimes I feel like a motherless child*
> *a long way from home . . . a long way from home.*

For them, God has a promise that can be downright miraculous once it penetrates and gets into their hearts and minds. It is news set like a diamond on velvet in the very first book of the Bible. Familiar almost to the point of being threadbare, it is a thunderclap that can set a life in a whole new direction! And it comes rolling out of those few verses in the first and second chapters of Genesis:

> *Then God said, "Let us make man [a person] in our image, after our likeness; and let them have dominion over the fish of the sea, and over the birds of the air, and over the cattle, and over all the earth, and over every creeping thing that creeps upon the earth." So God created man in his own image, in the image of God he created him; male and female he created them.*
> (Genesis 1:26-27)

> *. . . then the Lord God formed man of dust from the ground, and breathed into his nostrils the breath of life; and man became a living being.* (Genesis 2:7)

If there is any message that these verses has for any of us, it is that *we belong,* absolutely and forever, *to the God who in an act of will chose to fashion us to be his own!* Look at the text of Genesis, and you will see that the creation of human beings comes after God had made an inspection tour of everything else he had made. While he keeps declaring that what he produced is "good," among it all he found nothing that was enough like himself so that he could love it, and be loved by it, and the two of them could belong, and know that they belonged, to one another.

That is why God sits down, and in an awesome and tender act of creation, with his own hands, brings into existence the beings for which he one day would be willing to lay down his life rather than lose them.

Advent, Christmas, and Epiphany

To capture the wonder of that act, you need to get the picture of God birthing Adam in his hand. Much of the beauty and power of the scene are hidden in translation. Throughout most of Genesis, when God gets to the act of creating, he seems to do it from the divine throne by memo! "Let there be . . ." he says, and what he wants there "is"! First comes the order . . . then "POW" . . . the effect, without God ever soiling his hands in the effort!

But when it came to producing the human beings, a whole new tack was taken. To bring them into existence, God followed up his desire to have them appear by taking up the substance from which they were to come in his own hands, and doing the fashioning personally. The Hebrew terms that describe the process highlight that fact. The most common term used in Genesis for God's creative activity is *barah*. It is used only for the work of the Lord, and not for human activity. But it is a general term that refers to the run-of-the-mill productions of God. When God is *intimately caught up in fashioning something,* another word is used to depict him at work. *Yatzar,* "to fashion as a potter," is employed to describe a kind of labor that has to be "hands on" if ever it is to get done.

Have you ever watched a potter at work on his or her wheel? It is a sensuous, attention-demanding, finger-taxing enterprise that does not happen by chance. To get it all started the potter must pick up the clay, hoist it onto the wheel, push and work it to the center, then set the wheel in motion. Then, with that all done, he or she must fix head and heart, as well as fingers, on the object to be fashioned from his or her vision for it.

As the wheel spins, the clay takes on life under the potter's pressure. It grows and bulges, or is tucked into and pulled into contours it never had as a mere "lump." Changes are worked into it as the potter sees possibilities for it that appeared only after he put his hands to it. And when it is finished the piece that sits before him has the *throw lines,* the *print of the potter's hands,* all over what he has made! It is unique in all the world, a one-of-a-kind. And what is even more important is that it is his!

The point of these accounts in Genesis is that God wanted and wants those he makes. Not just Adam and Eve, but every person, everywhere, and he cannot rest until they *know* that they are his. In God's heart there is no such thing as an unwanted being.

We may not be wanted by some of them.

Some may not be wanted by their parents.

Others may not be wanted by their children.

Some may not be wanted by society.

Some may not even want themselves.

But unless the Word of God is a lie, God wants all of those he has laid his hands on. And he wants you and me to be involved in telling that news to others!

The human beings who surround us are so precious that God has called us to gather them into the arms he is holding out to them. We who know we are his are called by him to help others know that they are his, and ours, and that they belong, too. If they have God's claim check stamped into their being, then every person has value beyond their power to comprehend it.

No matter what their skill levels, or physical capacities, or gender, or color, God has deemed each worth dying for. That is how much *worth* they have.

If *that* is true, then we can be the most *secure* persons in the world. The God who values us more than he does himself will never let down or abandon us, even if everyone else we know does.

If *that* is so, then we have a *purpose* in life. It is to spread the Word and open the way for that Lover of a God to reach through us to others who are dying to know that this is true.

As the church, we are to be God's proxies to a world longing to experience and believe this good news. To get the message across takes *words* and *actions.* We all need to *hear* and *feel* that we are wanted. When individuals enter our gatherings in churches like this, we need to reflect to them what motivated us to want to touch their lives in the first place.

If people really matter, it should be impossible for them to enter and leave a congregation without contact and demonstrated concern. When a visitor appears, you will simply make it your business to stop by and meet them, and get to know their name, and let them know personally that you care that they came here, and will be eager to have them back if that possibility can present itself. Many are searching for a group of people with whom they can belong. You can be their proof that their search has come to an end.

If people *belong* to us as well as to God, then when they are hurt or are in need, we will surround them in a circle of love. With our resources and our time, and our bodies, we are challenged by God to make a difference in people's existence and in our world. We are to be help providers, and hope givers, who, if this fellowship were suddenly to disappear, would leave a gaping hole for all around us.

The crux of the matter is this: We have been brought together by God not only to be *brothers* and *sisters,* but *neighbors* to others, if they really have value and belong as we say they do.

That word *neighbor* in Greek is *plesion*. It means "to link up with, to draw close, to touch." It describes caring between people as it takes shape in day-to-day living. It reminds us that "neighborliness" takes time and effort and risk, and opens the possibility of rejection. It is the dogged effort to help people know, in tangible ways, that we love them.

If that inclusiveness, that "neighborliness," is not there for those lives which rub up against ours, then it would be better for them never to enter a place like this. All we will have done is hold out promises that we did not fulfill. What we usually end up with are disillusioned people who may come to believe that even the promises of God are not true because of how we have dealt with them. But it all *can happen,* and *will happen,* if you and I, together, *want* it to.

God so certainly wants it that he gave his people their commission to do that through the mouth of Isaiah:

> *"I am the LORD, I have called you in*
> *righteousness,*
> *I have taken you by the hand and*
> *kept you;*
> *I have given you as a covenant to the*
> *people, a light to the nations . . . ."*

Today the Christian family celebrates the Baptism of Jesus. That occasion marked the beginning of his public ministry, in which the words spoken by his Father through the prophet were brought

Do You See What I See?

to fruition. He has gathered us here for the *dual purpose* of recognizing that the Carpenter standing in the Jordan River, wet, is not only God's Son, but the Gatherer of God's people to move out with him on a divine mission . . .

> to help spread the gift of inclusion . . .
> to help bring those who stumble in their
> darkness into God's light . . .

to hold out hands to those who are "locked in," or "locked up," and lead them to the only One who can "set them free," indeed!

If we understand that, and act it out, then those who come through our doors, and into our lives, will know from those inside that she or he, at last, has been gathered in by the long arms of a Father. And once that happens, at last, their sense of loneliness can begin to fade, and their isolation and despair can start draining away. For they finally will be among "family," in whose midst the warmth, and love, and acceptance for which they desperately searched has been found.

Do You Hear What I Hear?

Epiphany 2   1 Samuel 3:1-10 (11-20)

The play is *St. Joan*. The year is 1429. The location is France. The setting is a castle where Charles, King of France, whose realm has been set astir by her activities and mystic visions, confronts Joan of Arc. The monarch stands before the little Maid of Orleans, trembling with rage. What has turned him into such a fury is the fact that God seemingly has had the audacity to select a nobody to become his vehicle for revelation in the land. Storming at his small, but uncringing subject, the obtuse king roars out in anger:

> "O your voices, your voices. Why don't the voices come to me? I am king, not you!"
>
> "They do come to you," replies Joan, "but you do not hear them. You have not sat in the field in the evening listening for them. When the angelus rings you cross yourself and have done with it; but if you prayed from your heart and listened to the trilling of the bells in the air after they stopped ringing, you would hear the voices as well as I."

And with that the nonplused king grits his teeth and clenches his fist.

Do You See What I See?

The place is Shiloh, a village about twenty miles north of Jerusalem. The year is about 1075 B.C., and the setting is the inner precincts of a shrine where the Ark of the Covenant is located. It is night, and an old priest named Eli and his young protege Samuel, are lying awake. Voices have been heard in their house, too, and those voices are at the center of their attention. Samuel is a lad who has been given by his parents to Eli for priestly training. The young man is dedicated and has learned enough to take his place beside his mentor so that, "Samuel was ministering to the Lord under Eli." (1 Samuel 3:1)

But on this night a new revelation has been interjected into that situation. A divine call has come to the youngster, waking him from his sleep. Unlike Joan, Samuel is not clear about who it is that he is hearing. Awakened a third time by the voice, he goes to Eli, supposing it is he who is beckoning to him out of the darkness. "Then Eli perceived that the Lord was calling the boy . . . ," and his teacher gives him his advice on how to respond should the voice come again. Hardly had Samuel returned to his bed when out of the still of the night ". . . the Lord came and stood . . . calling 'Samuel, Samuel.' " And the young man responds, "Speak Lord, for thy servant hears." What follows is an encounter between God and Samuel that changes the course of the latter's life and propels him into the midst of his people as a bearer of the divine Word.

What strikes me in that interchange is how willing Samuel was to take Eli's advice. Though the youngster had lived with the old prophet-priest long enough to know that God and his teacher linked up with each other, it was another matter entirely to have that happen to him! To catch that prompting from God needs an attentive and trainable ear. That, of course, is not an everyday combination, even for those who would love to possess it. Where do *you* go to find the voice of God these days, with so many voices speaking, many of which claim to be his? Can you expect to hear it as you "listen to the trilling of the bells after they stop ringing," or when you awaken from your sleep in the middle of the night? And if you do hear a voice coming out of either to you, how do you know it is God?

There are those who believe that if you are going to hear the Voice these days, you must go into the "fields of the world" filled

Advent, Christmas, and Epiphany

with the earth's masses. It will not be found where kings or presidents, or governments, or even churches are. God, they say, has stopped speaking in those "old order" places. God is to be found only where the action is. So the Voice of God, if you want to use the word "God" at all, is to be heard in involvement and activity.

Others believe it is to be found only in the sanctuary where the Ark and the Altar are located. To catch the nuances of God, one must run to the "Spirit Realm." It is in disengagement from the rumble of the world that God is to be heard. Involvement only muffles the Voice. Contemplation is the way to tune in to the Lord.

If we take Samuel's experience seriously, it is in *both* that the beckoning of God is to be expected. That understanding is wrapped up in the Hebrew word at the center of the experience, *shamah*. *Shamah* means "to hear, to listen, to catch the sound that beats upon the ear." It points out the fact that tuning in to God and being turned on by him demands that we open ourselves up to voices from outside of ourselves so that God has channels through which he can reach us.

Often the channels he most frequently uses are those that pass through other people on their way to us. God frequently makes his link-up through the mouths and lives of human beings whose lives rub up against ours. Those lives may be dressed like parents, or teachers, or peers, or individuals who float into and out of our existence. Or the Voice may come through persons who are physically dead and gone, but who themselves were so in touch with God that his Voice rings on even though they have stopped breathing. The Scripture is one of the places peppered with such channels of the Voice! The Bible is not a dusty antique that ought to be looked at as a curiosity piece. Though we often analyze it, dissect it, reconstruct it, and sometimes battle with it, it is more than just a piece of great literature. It is the diary of persons whose lives were sensitized to the working of God in their time and place. And the encounters that took place then have been preserved for the sharing in a variety of circumstances.

The Voice spoke encouragement in moments of stress and pain, "Be still and know that I am God." (Psalm 46:10) It sounded in time of oppression, "Let my people go!" (Exodus 7:16) It cut through to give directions for living when moral values had gotten

Do You See What I See?

fogged and misplaced, "You have been shown . . . what is good; and what the Lord requires of you but to do justice, and to love kindness, and to walk humbly with your God." (Micah 6:8) It gave assurance that life is not too big to handle, "I am with you always, to the close of the age." (Matthew 28:20) It brought words of hope when the future seemed to have been destroyed by the past, "Behold, I make all things new." (Revelation 21:5)

These words came from God through sensitive individuals, who though long dead, were real folks who lived in the real world! They are proof that the Bible does not pull people away from this world into a fairy-tale land, but is a channel for the Voice to flesh and blood individuals like ourselves surrounded by all the joys, trials and opportunities living has to offer. Through that contact point God reaches out to us in his efforts to make contact and move through his world with us in a vibrant, throbbing relationship.

For us to sharpen our own ears to that Voice, and dialog with this living, speaking Lord, we need to take seriously these other people who have been tuned in to and turned on by God before we have! They introduce us to the One who transformed and shaped their beings. Their broad witness to how God moves in his creation gives us clues to help recognize the *authentic* Voice when it sounds for us today. Listening to God as he comes through so many of these sensitized individuals helps us to learn the *accent* of the *divine* Voice.

In addition to the Scriptures, we have other aids for helping us recognize the Voice, in whatever form it comes. These are the history, traditions and confessions of the church. All of them help us translate the implications of the divine Word for the people who search for it in their day and age. Initially, they were born out of the quest for clues to the meaning of the Voice for themselves and their contemporaries. Then, having proved to be accurate descriptions of his revelations to them, they were passed on as guides to others who were on their heels in the same endeavor. They became something of a "spiritual road map" and a series of spiritual trail markers for the next wave of pilgrims. They remained behind to help those who followed to move forward in their journey with fewer chances of getting lost. Like other maps and sign posts they can be ignored or shunted aside so one can "do it" alone. But that is often foolhardy at best, and downright dangerous at worst.

I learned about the value of signs in unfamiliar territory one summer when I went with a relative to New Mexico. We had gone walking in the desert not far from a motel where we had stopped for the day. It was all gently rolling hills that lined the road and horizon. There was no apparent need to take the advice of the lady who checked us in that we had better take a compass with us if we left the paths. But "knowing better," and being venturesome, we headed away for the "untried!" In less than an hour of following our noses and the beautiful rock formations, we found ourselves in a maze of canyons that all looked alike. As the sun dipped over the horizon, we began to feel uneasy, then scared. Just as I was about to break into tears, my cousin noticed some writing scratched on a large stone over my head. The words were, "Como salir de aqui." "It's Spanish," he shouted gleefully. "It says, 'This is the way to go out!' We are heading in the right direction! Let's move!"

The confessions and creeds of Christendom are a lot like that sign. They point to directions taken by others who heard and followed the Voice, and who have shared their experience with us. We can go off entirely alone on our venture, turning off their assistance. But that would be foolish.

And we have the church to help us sort the voices that come to us, too. The church did not die in the First Century as it did not end when the last great creeds were written. There are people around us *now* who are as open to the Voice as were Eli, and Samuel, and St. Francis, and Martin Luther, and John Calvin, and an army of others who preceded and came after them. In tying in with them to listen, and share, and pray, and study, and labor and worship, we are more likely to catch the sound of that Voice than if we are off in the woods hugging a tree on our own! Together with the other listeners we can test out what we perceive by rubbing it up against the witness of others who have sought and heard the Voice. In that venture the *whole church,* not just an *elite corps* who want to think of themselves as the only true-blue "pick ups," can determine whether what we heard in fact was the Voice, or just ourselves singing in our "spiritual showers."

Do You See What I See?

But *shamah* does not have to do only with listening to sounds. That Hebrew term also means "to obey, to act." So when Samuel responded to the Voice calling out of the darkness, "Speak Lord, for your servant hears . . . ," he was not only telling God that he was *coming through loud and clear.* He was telling him that *he was ready to commit himself to the One who was speaking!*

As the prophets before and after him, and as Jesus was to do when he came, Samuel understood that God called for the handing over of the lives he touched. The punch line on each occasion when God got through to human beings was, "Come! Follow me!" Nowhere is that better summed up than in the ministry of the One who himself was the Word.

Jesus was constantly pushing people for decisions. He was One who couldn't rest easy with fence-sitters. He was always pushing them to jump for or away from him, even when they wanted to be faced with anything but a situation like that. His entry into Jerusalem on Palm Sunday was a case in point. Matthew tells us in his account about that incident: "And when he entered Jerusalem, all the city was *stirred,* saying, 'Who is this?' " (Matthew 21:10) That word translated "stirred" is the Greek term *eseisthe.* It means "an earthquake!" Jesus shook the city and those who populated it right down to their foundations, backing people up against the wall to decide Who it was Who was marching up to them, and what they were going to do with their lives now that he had.

He has done that same thing to others to whom he has called. You can bank on him doing it to you, too! *Christianity is not a philosophical head trip,* where those who have heard, and been intrigued by, the Voice can play around with it like a pile of blocks "out there," piling it up in different shapes *without ever having to decide* on what it is saying to, or asking from, them, then *giving themselves* to those calls. Christianity is an encounter with the Living, Enfleshed Word, Jesus Christ! And *that encounter forces us all to decide for or against him.* It pushes us to either throw in with him, with our whole beings, or leave him. It eventually sifts itself down to one basic question asked by Jesus to Peter, "Do *you* love me?"

Advent, Christmas, and Epiphany

If the answer is "Yes!" then we must link up with him and serve him, speaking unabashedly about our love for him . . . and following hard after him to give ourselves when, and where, and to whom he will show us. Where that commitment will take us we may not know at this moment. But this much is clear, it will involve moving out with Christ with *our feet* as well as *our hearts* and *minds*. Assuredly, as with Samuel and Joan and hundreds of millions of others, once that Voice sounds, we will have to put our lives on the line as we respond.

In *Habitation of Dragons*, Keith Miller retells Eldon Trueblood's story about a man who had the crazy notion to walk across Niagara Falls on a tightrope, pushing a wheelbarrow with a man in it:

> *He set two poles in his backyard, stretched a tightrope between them, and practiced every day for a year — first with a balance bar, then without it, then with a wheelbarrow, and finally he added a load of 175 pounds of bricks. And he never fell off the wire. His next-door neighbor watched every evening, and the crowds got larger every day as the time drew near. The press picked up the story, and when the big moment came, a huge throng was on hand. The fellow with the wheelbarrow appeared to be a little nervous as he stood looking out across the wire. He turned to his faithful neighbor and asked, "Joe, do you believe I can do it?"*
>
> *Slapping him confidently on the back Joe said, "I absolutely believe you can. I bet a tenth of this year's income on you."*
>
> *The performer looked out over the falls and then asked once more, "Joe, do you really believe?"*
>
> *Joe said seriously, "I really believe."*
>
> *"Fine," the other fellow replied, "you're my man. Get in the wheelbarrow."* (p. 35)

God always has a wheelbarrow in his hands as he calls to us. Whether it was to Samuel in the sanctuary, or to Joan in the trilling of the bells, or to Amos as he looked at a basket of rotting summer fruit, or to you and to me in whatever ways he has broken through to our awareness, God has the wheelbarrow in his hands. The Voice calls and once that Voice gets through things can never

Do You See What I See?

be the same again. *My life* and *yours* have reached their *watersheds*. God will not let go again. He will push us to open ourselves to him and to the task of assisting him in the reshaping of his creation. Since that is so, let's get busy obeying the call!

Disciple-Makers on the Way

Epiphany 3 *Jonah 3:1-5, 10*

The Epiphany season traditionally has been a time for renewed efforts in evangelism and Christian outreach. Emphasizing as it does the coming of the Wise Men to see the Christ Child, and their departing to tell the people of their homelands what they had experienced, the lessons which the church reads and ponders during the weeks of Epiphany focus on spreading the word of God's desire to embrace his world.

Old Testament Lessons like this one from Jonah tell how "... the word of the Lord came to Jonah the second time, saying, 'Arise, go to Nineveh, that great city, and proclaim to it the message that I tell you.'" God, speaking through the prophet, was out to lift the burden off the backs of folks who had tried walking through life without him.

Epistle Lessons like the one for today from 1 Corinthians (7:29-31) hold out appeals to a rebellious people and congregation in the name of Jesus Christ, for whom "... the appointed time has grown very short ... and this world is passing away," to let the Gospel pull them together and instruct a fractured bunch of converts.

Do You See What I See?

Gospel Lessons like today's from St. Mark (1:21-28) show us Jesus gathering about him the people whose lives will become intertwined with his forever:

> *And passing along by the Sea of Galilee, he saw Simon and Andrew the brother of Simon casting a net in the sea. And Jesus said to them, "Follow me and I will make you fishers of men."*

Then, three years later, as the capstone of his ministry among them, after his Resurrection, he gathers those two along with the others he recruited, before his Ascension to give them their final orders for carrying on that work of "fishing" for him in the world. With the moments fleeing like thieves, the time was at hand to put the work of drawing people to God into their laps. So, on a hilltop just across a creek from Jerusalem, huddled with the eleven he had left of his inner circle of followers, he put his mission design in their hands.

Jesus had come to earth through a stable to tell people about God, to lift them out of the misery and despair in which they had caged themselves. Then as he grew, by example and words, and vivid deeds, he had shown them the love God had for each. But the time came when spreading the news of his work had to be entrusted to human beings. And as that time came, Jesus pulled his followers together to tell them what they were to do in the days ahead. In a few words he placed in their hearts what General William Booth, founder of the Salvation Army, liked to call their "Marching Orders." He gave them the Great Commission to see that what he had done for humanity would be heralded throughout the world:

> *"Go, therefore, and make disciples of all nations, baptizing them in the name of the Father and of the Son and of the Holy Spirit. Teaching them to observe all that I have commanded you. And, lo, I am with you always, to the close of the age."*

It is important to note that Jesus did not give to the Apostles *instructions on how to organize boards and agencies to think up programs to promote!* Nor did he send them out to get busy on *a temple-building spree!* What he *did* was to point them toward

Advent, Christmas, and Epiphany

a personal encounter with people. As one human being to another, they were sent to tell the people of the world about what Jesus' coming meant for them. "Go make disciples," *he said. "You* go make disciples," is what *he meant!* He didn't *recommend* it, mind you. He did not *infer* it, you understand. He *ordered* it. He commanded that they go and do what he said, and do it beginning there and then!

Those last moment instructions should have surprised no one. All during his lifetime Jesus had been doing just that himself. The saving of human beings was his objective. The individual mattered. And he never allowed anything to separate him from those who needed what he alone had to give them.

It is important to remember what salvation meant in the language Jesus spoke. *Yasha* meant to "push back the walls," to "make space in which a person could move in freedom and safety," to "push back whatever threatened to destroy those who were being hemmed-in and crushed." At its center the word and activity had as their goal the freeing up of people to live in the here and now as well as in the eternity to come after they died.

It is also important to understand that the word for *disciple* in Greek, *mathates,* means to bring someone close enough to another so that he or she touches the teacher. It is hoped that *in the contact* that is so made, a bond is formed that can change and enlarge the student's life.

Notice how often Jesus did that personally while on earth. He reached out to *pull people close to him,* and *touched* them. The healing of lives that were broken or squashed occupied many of his waking moments. He went looking for such battered and hammered folks wherever they could be found. Almost always it was he who sought out the contact with the people. He did not wait in his carpenter shop for them to make an appointment. He packed up and went looking for those who needed him.

So it is no wonder that he told his friends to follow in the paths he had broken. *"Go to the people,"* he directed them, "You are going for me, but you are going *to the people* for them." And with his words in their ears, and his hand on their backs, the disciples went, as did generations of believers who followed, stretching in a "missionary line" from Jerusalem to here, where we live today!

Do You See What I See?

You see, that command of Jesus to "Go make disciples" is directed as much to you and me as it was to those eleven on the Mount of Olives. At our baptisms we were all ordained as evangelists, even if no halos were hung around our heads. The only issue that remains is how obedient we are to be to those "marching orders." To keep them in front of us is one of the reasons we celebrate the season of the Epiphany year after year.

The call of Jesus is underlined so persistently because the world eternally needs what you and I have to share with it. We are surrounded with people whose lives and destinies are in a needless shambles. They are inwardly curled up, disillusioned and guilt-laden; without the lifting power only Jesus Christ has they will forever be in a heap.

Simon Peter met such a person not long after he left that commissioning service. Entering the Temple mount, within earshot of where Jesus had started his evangelists marching, he was confronted by a crippled beggar being carried to the Golden Gate, where day after day he sat with a hand out for alms. Seeing the disciples he asked for a gift to help him eke out his existence. What transpired is a marvelous lesson on what evangelism is all about.

Instead of dropping a coin in a bowl and walking away to forget both the gift and the asker, Peter rivetted his eyes on the lame man's face. "Look at us," said Peter. And as the beggar raised his head the Apostle delivered his response: "I have no silver or gold, but I give you what I have; in the name of Jesus Christ of Nazareth, walk." Then, reaching down, he took the beggar by the hand and made him whole. Then off the man went with them into the Temple, says Luke, "walking and leaping and praising God."

I have stood on that very spot where the encounter took place. From it one can see the hill over which Jesus rode on Palm Sunday, and the Garden of Gethsemane in which he prayed on Maundy Thursday night. Turn 180 degrees and you can see the Church of the Holy Sepulchre, which covers Calvary where Jesus died on Good Friday. And at the foot of that hill lies the tomb from which he rose on Easter Day. *All in one turn of the body* you can see what happened in the life of the church *then*. And, as I have looked at it, I have thought of how different the church is now and yet how it is still the same.

Advent, Christmas, and Epiphany

It is *different* in that in its early days the Christian community, by and large, had, as Peter said, "no silver or gold," while today we possess and control wealth it is impossible to accurately tally. What is the *same* is that the deepest needs of the people we meet often can't be satisfied with what our money provides. After they are fed and supplied, a *different gift is needed* before they can get on their feet and go!

One of the greatest maladies we face these days is the sickness which loneliness and isolation have brought. The world seems to be filled wall-to-wall with people who are poverty stricken for mere human warmth and contact. Though there are more human bodies than ever walking the earth, we have learned that *proximity* does not equal *caring!* You can die of loneliness in a crowd.

That fact was driven home to me in a way that still makes my heart bleed. It came in a telephone call I got from a frantic father one Sunday evening. In desperation for some one to talk to, he had dialed the operator and had asked for the name of a minister who would come to his home. The operator on duty was a member of my parish. She gave him my number, and down to him I went. He lived in a six unit apartment building. When I got inside, the husband and wife, migrant workers in their late twenties, poured out the grief that had prompted the call in the first place.

They had been in town for seven months when their three-year-old son had become ill. Living on a shoestring, they had tried to treat him themselves. When he got worse, they took him to the emergency room at the hospital. There he had died early the next morning.

As is customary in Mexico, the body was brought back to rest in the house. A basket of flowers was set by the door, and a black wreath was hung over the mailbox. From the day it was there until I had been called two days later, not one person from the entire building had stopped by to lend a hand or say a word of comfort. "They had smiled," said the mother, "when they had passed us in the hallways on occasion. But then they ducked into their apartments and closed the doors. Our son never seemed to fit in with the rest of the children. The circles of friendship were closed. Even when the undertaker came and brought the casket home, they looked out of the windows from behind their curtains, but no one came to console us. We felt so deserted and alone."

Do You See What I See?

That happened not in some large city, but in a town of about twenty-five thousand people! And what happened then and there is not rare. People get shot and raped while others are standing by refusing to get involved. Not so much as a telephone is raised to summon help. That is because much of our society has become like gum balls in a vending machine. They touch, even bunch together, *but without intermingling.* They just clack up against one another, each inside of its own hard shell, insulated against the rest.

This goes on *despite a universal longing to have someone care and be "with" us.* We all need that. We all want warmth, whatever we may say to the contrary. What often happens is that one disappointment after another comes our way when we reach out for it, and we draw back and play it safe, and keep our distances. In doing that we shrivel a little at a time. And we become emotional cripples sitting by the roadside with our beggar's bowls in our hands, as inside we starve.

Silver and gold won't fill the bill, though we think on occasion they would do the trick and put us on our feet, if only we had enough of them! What we are reaching for is the demonstration that we are loved and cared about in *tangible* ways. And, until those things come, most human beings never get the strength to rise and walk through life healthy and whole.

That is why the response of Peter to that man by the gate is so vital for us to understand. In speaking the command to him, "in the name of Jesus of Nazareth, walk," Peter, as a human being, was reaching out as Christ's representative to make that very thing happen. Through his warm, earthy hands, he was linking *up to another needy human being.* When those hands met, God made a contact that had miraculous consequences!

The word "evangelism" has that kind of intent built right in. It comes from the Greek term *evangellion,* which means "good news." It is marvelous news to learn first-hand that God cares enough to lay his hand not just upon human life in general, but upon *your life in particular.* And the signs that *he is here to do that* often comes *dressed as you and me* as we follow his orders to carry the good news to help and care when all else, and everyone else, has fallen away.

Evangelists are also called to help people rise and walk away from *purposelessness,* as well. That is one of the other demons of the day that gnaws away at our lives. It shreds us by eating away any sense of our self-worth, driving us into a life of hell of having to justify our right even to stay alive. Though arrogance is a problem with which some people have to battle, the most pervasive enemy we have is the constant sense of put-down that is dumped on us from one place after another. Whether it is children constantly reproached as "stupid" by their elders, or adults being badgered as failures or foul-ups by their employers, we seem to spend much of our lives in a kind of hamster cage, running on wheels that we must turn in order to prove that we can keep up and somehow justify our existence. This treadmill running ultimately is a losing effort because the time inevitably comes when our speed and productivity fall off, our bodies slow down and the exactions of time begin to take their toll. When compared to others turning their wheels, we look like candidates for a shameful junk-heap of liabilities for society.

You can see it in the eyes of many of those who are less well equipped for the *giving of things* to the world. The aged, the poor, the handicapped are often looked upon with a sigh. Frequently they are ostracized, put out of sight and closeted, abandoned as embarrassments to the rest of us. We ghettoize them, or drop them off in retirement homes. And we leave them there to turn into nonpersons or zombies, knowing in the pit of our stomachs that someday we will likely join them.

I am often with those whom society and their families try to bury. They sit and stare and pine away, alone. They have nothing left to give that anyone else wants. So they are dumped. Then they drop like so many leaves from the trees in autumn, and wait to be raked up and hauled away.

What helps to destroy them, and each of us in our turn, is *what they come to think of themselves,* as well as *what others communicate by word and action.* They often buy the premise that their value, my value, as a human being depends on what we give or do. We are to be weighed and measured, and finally stamped with *worth* according to the height of the pile of money we made, or the goods we produced, or the college degrees we earned, or the

Do You See What I See?

titles we have had bestowed upon us. And those who don't have them to show are failures and no-accounts!

To those smothered by that load, evangelists are sent to minister! What we are sent to offer to them is as simple as it is profound. It is the "good news" declared in both words and symbols, so that if you can't *read* or *hear* them, you can *see* and *feel* the wonder of them anyway.

The words are from the mouth of the "evangelist sender," Jesus himself: "Come unto me all who labor and are heavy laden and I will give you rest." (Matthew 11:28) It is an open invitation, without qualification, without prerequisite. In fact, it has a special tag on it for those who seem to be the least worthy in the world's scheme of things. It is those with *loads* to *carry,* not *gifts* to *give,* that Jesus is calling to him with great persistence.

The symbol for that "good news" is from his life. It is the Cross on which he climbed to die for all people, productivity and successfulness be hanged! He said before he was nailed to it that it would be his gift to every human being: "I, when I be lifted up from the earth, will draw all men to myself." (John 12:32) Around its base space is available for *us all* on *equal footing.* When we stand there, as one day we all must, it is there that we learn, with ultimate clarity, that we are equally valued by the One above all of our heads!

Because they help to graphically drive that point home, I love bright brass processional Crosses! In their polished beams one can see, as they pass by, the reflections of the type of people loved by God. *It includes everybody it can reflect!* Your face and mine are there among the many. It radiates the truth that we all are precious to the One whose throne it was! It reminds us as it moves among us, that everyone of us bears the highest price tag ever paid by anyone for anything in the universe!

The faces of people from every nook and cranny of the world is what God always has wanted to see in the crowd of people gathered to call him their God. Whether Ninevah in the time of Jonah, or Judea and Jerusalem in the time of the Apostles, or the people of this city, the next country, or on the farthest flung continent in our day, God wants the ingathering to go on! And because the world is fuller than ever with persons still in such need, in this Epiphany season the call is made again for evangelists, "good news" bearers, to join the efforts of those first eleven. *This time,* as the command goes out, *your name* and *mine* are on the marching roster:

> *"Arise, go . . . and proclaim the message that
>   I tell you!"*

The Word of the Lord Came...

Epiphany 4   *Deuteronomy 18:15-20*

A few years ago, while I was visiting Boston, I wandered into a store that displayed a wonderful collection of posters. My eye happened to notice one poster hanging above the entrance, which the artist had entitled "The Making of a Prophet." It was a humorous scene depicting a scrawny lad almost knocked flat by what was happening to him. With his knees sagging, his mouth agape, and his eyes nearly bulging out of his head, he was gazing up at a cloud suspended overhead, out of which lightning was flashing.

In the center of the cloud one could make out an eye, and a voice was radiating from the mist. Transfixing the newly-made prophet, the voice boomed out, "Well then, my son, having said 'Yes,' how would you like to have your goose cooked now?"

While that poster and its quip do not present a verbatim account of the making of any specific prophet, at least as the Bible records it, the cartoon does depict some of the aspects that surround the summoning of those persons. As our Old Testament Lesson for today emphatically points out, the prophetic call did come from God, and the message delivered was, indeed, the Lord's. Moreover, the position did involve goose-cooking on more than one occasion. In addition, those who received the call from God were often the most surprised that, of all folks available for such a

Do You See What I See?

commission, God should have singled them out for so arduous and awesome a task.

Each of these aspects needs to be kept in mind when we listen to the messages of the great prophets who lived and labored nearly twenty-eight hundred years ago, or to ones purported to come from prophetic mouths in our own time. To do that, it is important to take an overall look at the basic characteristics of the Old Testament prophets as a group. Individuals all, each with unique traits, there were a number of similarities which they all shared and which set them apart as peculiar spokespersons for God, and which can give us a "grid" by which to sift out true prophets from the fakers today.

If there is one characteristic common to all biblical prophets, it was their absolute assurance that *God had called them personally into his service.* The Hebrew term which we translate into English as "prophet" is *nabi.* In its root sense it means "the one who was called." In every instance, that call was understood by the persons who received it to have been a *divine one.* When it came to the making of a prophet, *no human selection committee was involved* in the appointment of any of these speakers for the Lord.

As even a quick reading of their books reveals, the specific calls came to the various prophets in a variety of ways. Jeremiah, for instance, understood himself to have been ordained by God before his conception to be "a prophet to the nations." (Jeremiah 1:5) Amos, on the other hand, was a herdsman and a tender of "sycamore trees," whom God ordered to "go, prophesy" when Amos was an adult. (Amos 7:14-15) The great Isaiah was serving as a priest when he heard God's call for a messenger during a temple service. (Isaiah 6:1-8) Hosea, a family man, received his call through his personal crisis and marital difficulties. (Hosea 1:1-11)

Despite all of this diversity, each person understood his selection somehow to have been a divine one. The only self-made or self-determined prophets in biblical history were those who proved to be false ones. The mark of each true prophet was that he or she had a personal experience with God, though not always knee-buckling in character, that proved that God, and not someone else, had chosen him or her for the task. Hence, in a very special sense, right from the beginning, the prophets understood themselves to be *God's handpicked spokespersons* and *his personal messengers.*

Advent, Christmas, and Epiphany

The *prophetic utterances,* likewise, were understood by them to be God's words, not the prophet's own concoctions. Although the voice did not always come to the prophets out of a cloud, their words were not sermons which the prophets composed and then delivered to their contemporaries in God's behalf. Time and again, the prophetic speeches are introduced with such telling statements as "This is the message which the Lord gave Hosea . . ." (Hosea 1:1) "God revealed these things to (Amos) about Israel . . ." (Amos 1:1) "This is the message which the Lord gave to Micah . . . ." (Micah 1:1) to verify that God, not the prophet, was the author of what was about to be said.

Only when such divine messages were received did the true prophet speak, act, or write. In fact, there were periods of silence for all of the prophets, as the short length of most of their books attests. As Jeremiah reports, he had to wait ten days on one occasion before the Lord gave him the answer to an issue he had posed, and to which he wanted a response to deliver. (Jeremiah 42:1ff) Indeed, one of the signs of a self-appointed, and therefore false, prophet was that he or she acted and spoke without God's appointment and prompting. (Jeremiah 14:14-15) Such antics resulted in such people giving "a lying vision, worthless divination, and the deceit of their own minds." (Jeremiah 14:14)

The third characteristic of prophetic messages and the prophets themselves was that both were *radically conservative* ethically, socially and theologically. Contrary to many recent opinions, the prophets were not persons who broke with their religious traditions and then challenged others to bury their heritage with them. The fact is that the prophets were staunch advocates of the religious heritage from which they sprang, and continually called upon their contemporaries to embrace and live out the values they had been taught by God long before, values which they personally had promised to incorporate into their own lifestyles. It is true that the prophets were radicals in the core sense of the word. They drove to the root of the issues that confronted them in their ministries, which is what the term "radical" means. They were driven to deal with the heart of the problems that beset society, not just to play with the peripheral issues.

Moreover, *they did so as members of the believing community,* calling to errant brothers and sisters in the same faith tradition to reform and live out their lives in line with the Word of God given through the ages. It is a mistake, therefore, to depict the prophets as wild-eyed loners standing outside of the fellowship of Israel, addressing an "alien" group, hopelessly trapped by outdated "traditions." If anything, *the prophets saw themselves as belonging to the people to whom they were called to minister.*

This is an extremely important point to keep in mind in an age when we are bombarded by individuals who would tell us that being prophetic means setting oneself against and apart from, the organized church or traditional faith community. They would have us believe that even to identify oneself as a member of that faith community is repugnant to the Lord! Such an attitude was foreign to the prophets who, in Deuteronomy, God promised to raise up! While thundering for change within society and individual lives, they pressed God's case as members of the religious community they were challenging. For *it was that believing community,* which for all of its distortion, and failures in the past, that produced the very ones God called to be his prophetic messengers! It was through Israel that God sorted when he was selecting the appropriate people to be his spokespersons.

The prophets did not drop from heaven on parachutes or hatch in strange lands under rocks. They arose from the people of God, where they most often had been bred, nurtured, trained, and at times even supported in their work. As they carried out their missions, they drew upon the religious heritage which they held in common with the people to whom God had sent them, as Micah himself pointed out when he stood and preached to the people of Israel:

> [The Lord] has told us what is good. What he requires of us is this, to do what is just, show constant love, and humbly obey our God. (Micah 6:8)

Micah, as would be true of his prophetic colleagues that followed him, rarely delivered *new* or *novel* messages to his hearers. The Word that God moved him and them to speak was a word

Advent, Christmas, and Epiphany

which most of the people had heard many times before. What the prophets were called to do was, as one Israelite to other Israelites, move their people to be faithful to a heritage they together professed and which they had sworn to obey in dealing with God and each other. The prophetic challenges for the *future* continually were made on an appeal to *their common traditions* which God was pressing them all to enflesh anew. That call for personal renewal was radical in its efforts to conserve what was best for society based upon their experience with God.

A fourth characteristic of the prophets was that *they generally were laypersons*. Except for Moses, Isaiah, Jeremiah and Ezekiel, all of the other prophets, as far as we know, were laypeople. Whether these spokespersons of the Lord continued to function in their normal trades alongside of their prophetic ministries is not usually revealed in their books. Judging from the few sermons or acts contained in the writings attributed to them, it appears probable that either their prophetic occasions came as scattered periods in their day-to-day functions or that their prophetic careers were short-lived, being confined to a few years, or even weeks, during which they left their homes and trades to speak and act for the Lord.

Apparently not many of the prophets lived happy lives, at least not in the generally accepted sense of that term. Hosea's home was torn by the adultery of his wife. (Hosea 3:1ff) Amos faced opposition from the priest Amaziah, who went to the king with his charges of sedition against the prophet. (Amos 7:10ff) Jeremiah was ostracized by his contemporaries, forcing him to cry out in his loneliness. (Jeremiah 12:7-11) He later was publicly humiliated and branded as a traitor, being thrust into prison for his efforts at saving the nation.

One of Jeremiah's contemporaries, a prophet named Uriah, fared even worse. He was put to death by King Jehoiakim, who murdered him with the royal sword for preaching essentially the same message in Jerusalem which Jeremiah himself proclaimed. (Jeremiah 26:20) Jesus later was to sum up this lot of the prophets when he looked over Jerusalem during his processional entry into that city and wept:

> *O Jerusalem, Jerusalem, killing the prophets and stoning those who are sent to you! How often would I have gathered your children together as a hen gathers her brood under her wings, and you would not!* (Luke 13:34)

Do You See What I See?

The lives of most of the prophets probably were difficult because the messages God delivered through them placed them frequently in opposition roles in relationship to their contemporaries. Being sent by God to challenge corruption among the common as well as the mighty people meant for most of them being met with hostility and rage on the part of the persons whose sins they fingered. Despite such attitudes, one of the distinguished traits of the vast majority of biblical prophets was that *they continued to love the people they addressed* regardless of the popular response to them. This held true even for those difficult situations when their preaching fell on apparently stopped-up ears.

With Hosea as one of their outstanding examples, *the prophets tended to be forgiving and hopeful,* despite the fact that they had few apparent reasons for being so when they looked for potential change in the lives of the people they engaged. Their messages are shot through with the optimistic call for people to remake their lives. If that call is to be taken seriously, then we must assume that *the prophets believed that the people to whom they preached could in fact alter their conduct.* If that were true, then the chance for changing the course of an individual life, a community, or a nation always existed, no matter how depressing the future appeared to be.

The prophets clung doggedly to the conviction that even a badly corrupted social order had the potential of being turned around with God's help, and the willingness of the people to take advantage of that chance for a new day which the Lord continually provided for them. This is one of the main reasons that even the most gloomy of the prophets, such as Amos, has rays of hope for a better tomorrow shining through his most dour warnings of potential catastrophe. Even the harsher predictions of doom are usually couched in settings of possible restoration. And it is this combination of *confrontation* and *compassion* which, I feel, has kept the prophets in the forefront of our religious heritage.

Because these spokespersons for God all saw life without misty-eyed illusions, their value has not faded through the thousands of years that separate them from us. The situations they addressed remain with us still, merely updated and dropped into contemporary settings.

Advent, Christmas, and Epiphany

This being so, the prophets are not just *fixtures from* and *for the past.* But they, and their more contemporary successors, still are able to walk up and tap us in our consciences, probing us to get our lives in order individually, with one another, and with the Lord who made and loves us all.

Keeping Up the Pitch

Epiphany 5   *Job 7:1-7*

During one of the most productive periods of his literary career, the famous writer, Robert Louis Stevenson, was living on his island retreat, working on a book. For months he had been pouring out his story at break-neck pace, when suddenly his inspiration seemed to dry up. For weeks he struggled to regain his form, to no avail. Finally in a fit of desperation he wrote to his closest friend, "Tell me, Malcom, if you can, how can I keep up the pitch?"

When Stevenson wrote that letter he could have taken as his text the words of Job:

> *Has not man a hard service upon*
>   *earth,*
> *and are not his days like the days of*
>   *a hireling?*
> *Like a slave who longs for the*
>   *shadow,*
> *and like a hireling who looks for his*
>   *wages,*
> *so I am allotted months of emptiness,*
>   *and nights of misery are apportioned*
>   *to me.*

Do You See What I See?

> When I lie down I say, 'When shall I
>   arise?'
> But the night is long,
>   and I am full of tossing till the dawn.
> My flesh is clothed with worms and
>   dirt;
> my skin hardens, then breaks out
>   afresh.
> My days are swifter than a weaver's
>   shuttle,
>   and come to their end without hope.
> Remember that my life is a breath;
>   my eye will never again see good.

And, frankly, given the right day and hour, most of us could have added our, "Amen!" Is there *anybody* who *hasn't felt this way* more than once?

You see, keeping up the pitch and fighting off despair is not just a problem of writers and artists. It is a battle for us all. Whatever we do or undertake, be it a business venture, a personal enterprise, or just the day-to-day living of our lives, the time inevitably comes when we become bogged down with the feeling of despair and disillusionment.

Recently I got home in the early afternoon, following an exciting luncheon meeting, and sat down at my desk to start work on this sermon. A few minutes into the effort the telephone rang, and at the other end of the line was a young couple I had never met, but who were in a deep crisis in their lives. Without giving me their names, they said they had met someone who had told them to call me to see if I could help. To protect their anonymity, they used the phone to make the contact.

For two hours, with them on both their telephone extensions, they told me how just a couple of years ago they had been a buoyant pair of youngsters. They had had a lovely courtship and life was heady as they walked to the altar. Then they were off on a honeymoon, ala the bridal magazines. After that it was back to a newly furnished apartment still filled with the love and joy that surrounded the first blush of marriage.

Advent, Christmas, and Epiphany

But after only a few months together things began to change. The stars in their eyes began to fade and sparks began to fly. They began to grate on each other. The husband chided the wife that she was not what he thought she would be. She was not as prim and "sporty" as she had been when they were dating. He had had enough of making breakfast for himself and seeing her hair up in curlers. The wife had had her fill of him, too! He was not the boy she thought she had married. Then, she never had to push him to shave or change his shorts. Where were the nights out and time to be spent alone? In short, all of the glamor that had wrapped up their portrait of matrimony soon had become tarnished when they settled down to the day-to-day problems of living with each other, faults and all!

And marriage isn't the only institution where life can have the air let out of it. There seems to be nothing that is off limits for the infectious germ of despair. Each of us, at one point or another, is going to have our existence, even in areas we love, lose its tang and become a drag! A lot of picky issues, interspersed with the crushing issues of life which we all deal with eventually, have a way of wringing us out and leaving us feeling depleted.

Look where you will, and you will see folks "popping their corks" in every walk of life. The week after Christmas I had a letter from a former student of mine, now a pastor in his mid-thirties, who was writing from a hospital room where the pressures he faced daily had put him. That is not unusual any more. The problems you and I haul around in our society make us feel as though we are living under the thumb screw, whatever we do.

People in business frequently live under continual pressure to produce more and more. Thought of as soft-bodied robots, they are run at frantic speeds until they break down. Then they are replaced by another like them . . . and that is that!

Homemakers often blow their gaskets under the relentless routine of the constant demands and frequent boredom of the household. They labor at dozens of unrelenting chores while the walls seem to be on wheels, rolling ever closer, like a squeeze cage, apparently with no reverse gear!

Do You See What I See?

What makes the situation all the tougher is that people get so discouraged that they begin to think that they are all alone in their distress. This loneliness, often silently borne, has become one of the crucial problems of our time.

People feel more isolated from one another at the very time that the population is becoming crushingly large! Almost daily, better ways of communication are discovered. There are more people per square foot, and more ways for getting in touch with them, than ever before. And yet for all of this, too many appear to be in transparent cocoons, speeding past one another so fast that we seem increasingly less able even *to notice* the other being, *let alone connect* with them! People are in such a hurry that we pass each other in a blur. Individuals are becoming just a kind of graffiti on our psychological walls . . . ignored and lonely.

We are finding that there really is no consolation in the crowd. Individuals have their own problems and don't want to take on any others. So, though each would like to have the warmth and friendship of his or her neighbor, we usually feel it is better to leave well enough alone. Even when friendships do develop, many remain superficial. They seldom get beyond the surface niceties. The main reason for that, I think, is that we are afraid of what it will cost us to get committed and involved.

To find relief from the anxieties, these lonely troubled souls try everything from the latest fad in group therapy to extra-marital flings and mood bending substances which any bottle, capsule, straw or needle can provide for them. They are willing to experiment with almost anything to get the high that comes from feeling part of a group that cares. And in some instances, for a while at least, they find something of what they seek. But too often what they find is that really none of the group really *belongs* to the other because each is only trying to *get something for him or herself.* And since each one is trying *to get* without having *to give* themselves in return, then belonging becomes a state that simply cannot exist. To *belong,* two people must reach out to each other and open themselves to making a connection that will last longer than the instant in which a leech clings to its prey before dropping off in search of its next victim!

Advent, Christmas, and Epiphany

It is tough to find such reaching, such willingness to link up, even in many families. I saw just how tragic it can be at times early in my ministry when I worked with a group of psychiatrists and patients at a mental hospital near the parish I served. One of the patients with whom I dealt was a seven-year-old boy who was so disturbed that for a long while he would communicate with no one. He seemed to be in a state of bottomless depression. He would sit and stare out of the window of the ward where he was taken every morning and afternoon, clutching a large rag doll he had brought with him when he was admitted.

One day I saw him go through a ritual which his therapist had called me to observe. It was as fascinating as it was heart-tearing. After he had sat on the floor for a long while, he would take the doll and prop it up against the wall across from the window. Then he would pull out the legs and straighten the doll's skirt. That done, he would sit down on its lap, pulling its arms around his waist. Then, laying his head on the doll's shoulder, he would rock, humming softly to himself. Then he would get up and go back to the window and stare out in silence.

The child had come from a well-to-do family. He was an only child who had at his fingertips all that the family's money could buy for him, everything from a pool to a pony. What he did not have was his parents' touch.

They had provided for a series of nurses to care for him while they were out or away from him. They sent him on trips and swamped him with toys, even on non-important days! But each was so caught up in the whirl of their own lives, so crammed full of personal "needs," that they never had the time, or never had learned, to
      rock him to sleep themselves . . .
          or scoop him up and plant him on their laps and hug him. They never even had time to paddle him! He never knew what it was to be held and kissed by them without reason. So he had built a dream world where he could find what he missed where he lived. He sought in a *doll* and *the depths of his imagination* what he had been denied in reality . . . the warmth of someone whose caring he could experience and understand. Because it had become so painful to "keep up the pitch" of living he had drifted off into his world of fantasy.

Do You See What I See?

As I worked with his parents, I learned that it was not that they did not love him! They did, in their own ways. What they had failed to do was find *ways of showing it in terms he could understand.* They had tried to use *things* to do what only *two arms and time* can accomplish!

Human beings need to know that they matter . . . we really do! We need to know that we are loved . . . that is a fact. And we need to have those realities expressed in *concrete ways.* We are so built that to "keep up the pitch" in life we must have tangible, visible demonstrations of the fact that someone really does care.

Oh, we can deal with love as an *idea.* We can define it, and analyze it, and argue about it. But for it to make *any difference,* to become effective, *we must have it shown,* and *show it ourselves,* in shapes that can be *seen* and *felt.*

Thousands of families and individual lives would be held together and made fuller and more liveable if love were demonstrated more often. Veritable miracles can take place in the healing of relationships if:

> husbands would take the time to wrap their wives up in their arms and tell them that they love them after the courtship is over . . .
>> wives would take the time to let their spouses know that they mean more to them than an insurance policy against poverty . . .
>>> parents would put into words for our children the love bond that actually exists between us . . .
>>>> children would grasp the moment to express in tangible form the affection they have for us so that we could hear it while we are alive, instead of us both having to grieve about it because it was lost in silence during the here and now!

In so many cases, such love is taken as a matter of fact which the other person should understand and accept without its having to be acted out!

We husbands assume that our families know how we feel because we work every day and hand over the paycheck. Wives, in

Advent, Christmas, and Epiphany

turn, are certain that their love is apparent when the meals are on the table and the clothes are on hangers in the closet. And children, well, with cards now and then, and flowers on the big days, all that needs to be demonstrated has been taken care of, right? All the while each of us is waiting, and wants, to know that we matter to the other! We wait to be shown that *we are loved for ourselves* more than for the services we provide to each other.

In his words to his people, long before Jesus was born, the prophet Isaiah pointed out how God demonstrated his love for those he cherished:

> *"Be strong," he told Israel, "fear not!*
> *Behold your God will come . . .*
> *He will come and save you."*

While the Lord could have stood at the edge of the clouds and expected his people to know that they mattered to him because the rains came . . .

    and the sun shone . . .

        and their hearts kept beating . . .

            and the earth produced to feed and house them . . .
he actually came to the planet and *spoke to them* so they could know, individually that it was he who really cared!

He came to Moses up on the hillside in the wilderness so they could meet up close, face-to-face.

He came down to the streets and roads of Palestine to rub shoulders with the crowds that came to meet the Carpenter from Nazareth. And after his arrival, notice how often Jesus appears in the Gospels moving in *close enough to touch the people* and *to be touched by them*. It was in the *touching* that

        deaf-mutes had their ears opened and tongues set free . . .

            sick people of all descriptions had their bodies fused and recharged . . .

                people given up for dead were given new life . . .

                    and hopeless folk, who couldn't "keep up the pitch," like Zacchaeus, and

Do You See What I See?

Levi, and Mary Magdalene, and scads of others like them, but who are forever unnamed, were remade and set loose with joy in their steps again!

You see, in the physical, up-close ways where they could feel his heart open up to them, the Lord made people blossom who were shriveling up inside until he made contact with them. In that *contact* he was showing us *how it is to be done:* "Speak out and touch someone with your love!"

Often his lesson in loving gets us anxious and up-tight. We feel awkward and self-conscious where tenderness is concerned. We get embarrassed and flustered about trying it because we are afraid that we will look silly, or mess it up.

But making love alive and visible is *simple*, if not easy . . . at least not easy at first. What you do is simply *say it* — "I . . . love . . . you . . . ." — and you say it even if your voice quivers and beads of sweat pop out on your head as you do! You *reach out* and *touch* the other person . . . even if the words you want to accompany it won't come, and your face flushes! It is these *acts* that link us up to each other. They tell those we love, and have loved, that we do, in terms that cannot be missed.

The first steps in acting out love are always the hardest. It is hard to break the ice — especially if opportunities to do it over the years have been missed and allowed to slip by. But I have learned in my own life that love is like a blanket. When it is wrapped around those who matter to us, it can melt the ice of the past, letting those inside feel the warmth that tells them that we have claimed them as our own.

Nothing else that I have ever seen has such power as that to send a new zest surging through existence. Yes, the "nights of misery" are long, and we are "full of tossing till the dawn." But a new day is coming! God has promised it! And since that is so, "keep up the pitch" in the living of *your* days!

What Do You Do When the Raft Comes Apart?

Epiphany 6   *2 Kings 5:1-14*

Dr. Samuel Shoemaker, the famous Rector of Calvary Episcopal Church, Pittsburgh, Pennsylvania, and one of the greatest preachers ever produced in this country, was invited to preach at the chapel services at a well-known New England boys' school. He went in the autumn of the year, when the mountains and countryside were simply ablaze with color. After the engagement was concluded, the Head Master would not allow him to leave the premises until he had taken a complete tour of the campus.

As they walked through the fields, they reached a bluff overlooking a river which served as a property line. The Head Master turned and said to Sam, "You may have heard that we had a near tragedy down there just this past week. It could have been a disaster." Two of the youngsters, faced with exams, had tried to find a solution to the pressure they were feeling. Like Huck Finn, one of them had gathered some driftwood, while the other had gotten some old rope from the stable. Using the rope to bind the logs together, they made a raft and hopped aboard. Then, with a pole they had scrounged, they pushed out into the deep, confident that they had the avenue before them to leave their troubles behind.

But no sooner had they hit the center of the stream when the old rope broke, dumping them into the middle of the drink. "Both

Do You See What I See?

of those boys could have drowned," the Head Master snorted. Then turning to Sam he said, "When you get home, Dr. Shoemaker, how about preaching a sermon sometime on what you do when the raft comes apart."

A couple years later, standing in the Lutheran Cathedral in Hamburg, Germany, I thought about what that Head Master had said to Shoemaker. Ernst von Kempke, the organist of the church, was showing me the tryptic above the altar when a young girl came up to me. Tugging at my sleeve, she said, "I see by your collar that you are a clergyman, and I hear from your voice that you are an American. Can I talk to you for a moment?"

Once we sat down in one of the pews, she told me why she had pulled me aside. "I am on my way home from a visit to a clinic in Switzerland. They told me that I have a brain tumor that cannot be cured. I am only sixteen years old and have only about six months to live. What in God's name am I going to do?"

That was not the first time a person whose raft had come apart asked me that question. As a pastor and counsellor, I have met many folks in such a fix. What would you say to people in binds like that if you were in my shoes?

What would you say to a woman of fifty who had suffered a stroke so massive that all she could do was move the eyeballs in her head to count the seams in the wallpaper on her ceiling? She could no longer do the most elementary things in life for herself, and yet she might have many years to live. What in God's name was she supposed to do?

Or take a man who is thirty-six years old, with four young children, who comes home from work too early one afternoon and finds his wife in bed with a neighbor. His marriage has come apart. He has a family to raise and a business to run. What in God's name is he supposed to do?

Or sit in the kitchen with a fellow in the twilight of hireability who, after giving thirty-one years of his life to a company, is cut loose in a take-over reorganization with nowhere to go. He still has the power and the desire to be productive, but no one will hire him at his age. Like a sixth wheel for a wagon, what in God's name is he supposed to do?

Lives, of course, are not carbon copies of one another, so there is no "standard" answers to such crises. But there are two things that I have learned about life, and God, and ourselves, which once we understand give us a pair of handles to help us pull our rafts back together enough to get back on board.

The first of these handles is that *in the midst* of the trials and hellish situations into which we are thrown when the raft comes apart, *God is already present.* And what is more, he is there not as a *spectator* but as a *participant* who wants what is best for us, and who will give us what is best for us if only we will give him the chance.

Now this sounds nice, doesn't it, and it is the kind of thing you expect to have shoveled out of a pulpit on a Sunday morning. But can you bank on it, and operate on it in real-life whirlpools? Some say "No." They are like the fellow I met in the hospital one day when one of the members of my parish, who was the supervising nurse on duty, asked me to "look in." This man was terminally ill, and had had no other visitors except the staff during his entire hospitalization. Walking up to his room, I hardly had my head inside the door when he gave me "both barrels," reloaded, and gave them to me again: "I don't need anybody like you in here now. I know what I got and I have to go it alone. And anything you say to the contrary, buddy, is so much pious garbage."

I will always remember that fellow for his colorful language. What he said was not new. When we are hurt, we all want help *now*. And if it doesn't come, and *come in the shape we know it should,* then we, like that fellow, feel abandoned and alone and furious. We are in those fixes either because *God doesn't know* what has happened to us, or because *God doesn't care* what has happened to us, or because *there isn't any God* to know or care. If God were real, and caring, and anywhere in the vicinity, we wouldn't have been dumped into the drink. And we are so certain of this, when the rope breaks and our rafts come apart, because we have mapped out exactly how God should act if he were any of the above. Because, you see, we think *we know how we would act if we were God.* And, obviously, because he hasn't done it *our way,* he has simply abandoned us when we needed him most.

Do You See What I See?

Just watch how that works. Take the death of someone you really love. Someone whose life is so wrapped around you that when it is pulled loose it takes part of you with it, and you bleed. That kind of person. When that raft comes apart, you know that there will be no tomorrow worth the name. You are certain that life will never be worth living again. No one or thing will ever fill the void they have left, not ever again. And if someone comes up and puts an arm on your shoulder and says to you, "I know, but time will help you heal," you want to stick your fingers in their ears and tear their head off. You know that the only reason they said such a stupid thing is that they didn't know what else to say. You see, *if God had cared about you,* that raft wouldn't have come apart. And if he were near *now,* you would be able to *feel it.* That speech is so much "pious garbage."

But the fact is that time *is* a balm into which God already has dipped his finger. At that very moment, he is rubbing it gently into that wound, even while you are in the greatest pain. You may well be too numb to feel it, but he, in fact, is close enough to be doing that. But it may not be coming in the form you think you would provide it if you were God.

Or take the times of loneliness, frustration, fear and despair, which makes for so many of the emotional breakdowns of our day. Times like that make a body *feel* alone and isolated and adrift. If someone says that God cares, or that they, or some other human being cares, we don't believe it. If we believed *that* we wouldn't be in the fix we are.

But I have worked with such people often enough to know that when they realize that *our being there* is a sign that *we* care, and that the God who moved us to be there is also on the spot, caring and present even when we aren't, they are on their way out of the snake pit. But the problem for us all in the midst of so many of our raft break-ups is that God *seems* so distant when it comes apart . . . *because he is not there in the way we think we would be if we were God.*

That was the problem that Naaman had, you know. He was a man who had everything. He was Chief of Staff of the most powerful army in the world. He had so much influence with the King of Assyria that he could pull political strings with the throne to satisfy his personal needs on the spot. He had it all except . . . his health. Naaman became a leper, and what good was all the rest without a cure for that dreaded disease? He was in the same situation as we . . . what good is all the rest without the one thing . . . whatever it may be . . . that we want most when the raft comes apart?

But then Naaman heard from his maid that there was a person in Israel, a conquered province, who could pull his raft together. So, with a letter from the King of Assyria to the King of Israel in his bag, off he goes with a retinue of troops and servants befitting his status. And to get his heart's desire, Naaman goes wheeling up to the door of Elisha's house expecting a welcome, and a healing performance, worthy of his station.

But Elisha doesn't even come out of the house. He sends a servant with instructions for his visitor: "Go and wash in the Jordan seven times, and your flesh shall be restored and you shall be clean." What? No prophet coming out to wave his hand over the place . . . and call down some thunder and lightning . . . and zap a healing for him designed for a Chief of Staff? Just the second-hand order, "Go wash seven times in the Jordan?" In a fit of anger, Naaman determined to head for home.

You need to *see* the Jordan to understand Naaman's response. To call it a river is a generous exaggeration. For most of its length, it is a muddy creek only a few yards wide, and four or five feet deep. Naaman had better rivers back home. He was not going to walk into that cesspool and be made a laughing stock in front of his troops. Writing the whole venture off as a very bad mistake, he turned and "went away in a rage." But it was then that his servant sidled up to him and said: "If the prophet had commanded you to do some *great thing,* would you not have done it? . . . Wash."

So, grumbling under his breath about the stupidity of it all, to go wading into that God-forsaken mud puddle, and in front of his soldiers no less, Naaman plodded into the Jordan. He went in up to his ankles . . . then to his thighs . . . then, "bloop," he was in over his head. And when Naaman looked down at his hands as they came out of the water, they were as clean as the backside of a well-cared-for baby.

Do You See What I See?

God couldn't be in the middle of a muddy creek. *But there he was* . . . just *waiting* for old Naaman. God had been there with him all of the time, with all of his power, *even when he seemed to be nowhere in sight.*

You and I need to remember that when our rafts come apart, and we are caught in the middle of the stream of fear and pain. This is God's universe . . .

    we are his people . . .

        and he fills the one and loves the other . . .

Like a mother with a hurt child, he *never* lets us out of his conscious concern and care.

Just *how* and *when* he will respond to you when your raft breaks, only he knows. But any God who loved you and me enough to climb on a Cross and give his life for us will never let his hand slip from us when we are dumped into the middle of the stream. Of that we can be certain.

That is First.

Second, when the raft comes apart, and we hit the water, *we must swim to stay afloat.*

God, at the creation of the world generally, and at our births specifically, built into us marvelous floatation devices. He expects us to *use them* when we experience tribulation.

Jesus was very honest about life. That is why I trust him as well as love him. Looking into the toil-worn faces of weary folks who came to him for words of assurance, he said to them:

"In this world you will have tribulation."

That is not what they came to hear! They wanted him to tell them that he would save them *from* tribulation. But he was telling them the truth about living from step one.

    Throwing in with him carries no promises that you will not get cancer . . .

        or have a heart attack . . .

            or lose your job . . .

        or that your kids will not get into trouble.

Believing in him does not insulate us against the natural pangs of living.

Advent, Christmas, and Epiphany

But this same Jesus said to the same people:

"Be of good cheer, for I have overcome the world."

The assumption was that because he had, we could, too.

You see, Jesus gave no guarantees against the problems of life. What he did give us was a Cross-clad guarantee against *being drowned by them* when the raft comes apart . . . *if* we will *use his power,* and *ours,* to *fight back* and swim.

Some people never get enough of their raft back together to survive because they find it easier to sink than to swim. When the rope breaks, they "throw in the towel," or take an emotional gas pipe. They quit and await the "inevitable."

But others are like Ben Hur, in Lee Wallace's novel of the same name. A young Jew is condemned to be a galley slave because, by accident, a loose roof tile falls from where he is standing as an observer and kills a Roman Officer. Had Judah Ben Hur been a run-of-the-mill Judean, he would have been killed on the spot. But, because of his status as a member of a renowned family, he is sentenced to die out at sea, away from the eyes of his people. But the youth determines not to give up hope for freedom and a return home. He vows to struggle for his life.

Judah, like all the other condemned prisoners, is chained to the seat next to his oars. But he was unlike the rest of the rowers who, resigned to their fate, gave up hope and dropped daily from despair and depression, only to be tossed overboard as fish food. Judah, using the same adversity that killed them, got himself transferred from one side of the ship to the other. And as he sat in his irons in the belly of the ship, he pulled the oars with *determination* rather than *resignation.*

Then one day a sea battle erupted between the Roman fleet and their enemies. Judah's ship was rammed and sank. Freed from the wreckage of the doomed vessel, with the muscles he had built *at the hated oars,* he was able to swim with the weight of the chains that had bound him, to a piece of flotsam. From that piece of raft he was rescued, along with a Roman officer he had pulled to safety. He was taken to Rome, and on a momentous day won a victory in the chariot race that opened the way for him to go back to Judea. *Using his adversity rather than letting it destroy him,* Judah wrung from it new strength and another chance to live.

Do You See What I See?

For many of us, when the raft comes apart in life we, too, often give up at the oars. Instead of rowing, we waste our time incessantly asking the wrong kinds of questions . . . often those that can never be answered with any certainty . . . like:
"*Why* did *this* happen to *me?*"
The real issue isn't that at all. The question to be answered is:
"Now that this *has* happened, *what can I do with it?*"
When the raft comes apart, as it will many times before we die, it is frightening. I have been so scared at times that my brain has gone numb. But when we hit the water, *first call on God* for all we are worth and watch for his helping hand. But *then* we must *abandon our despair* and *get to work surviving.* For the hands through which God sends the help to get us out of the drink may be those he already has attached to our very own arms.

The story was told by Clement Atlee, the Minister of State for Great Britain during the Second World War, about a briefing session that was held in a bunker in London when things were at their worst for England. Bombed day and night, it appeared that the Germans were preparing to send in paratroops and start an invasion which seemed to have a real chance of spelling that nation's doom.

> *As we sat around the table giving him our direst predictions, Churchill just sat there with that big cigar clenched between his teeth. When we were finished we turned for his response. For a moment he just sat in his chair, loooking at the ceiling. Then he rolled back in his seat, took the cigar out of his mouth and said,*
>
> *"You know . . . I find it all rather inspiring."*

You and I can't always control what comes our way. Nor can we always keep our rafts from coming apart. But we have a lot to say about what will happen once they do. If we choose, we can face our trials with *fear* and *dumb resignation* . . . or like Naaman, *we can head for help, link up with the power of God* who makes all things possible, and *swim for all we are worth.* If we do *that* when the rope breaks, and the raft comes apart, what we inevitably will find is this . . . that God will turn our suffering into the anvil on which an even greater saint, literally, is being pounded out.

The Now and Yet is What to Be

Epiphany 7   Isaiah 43:18-25

There are times when to practical people the Bible seems to be talking out of the top of its head! The claims it makes or the advice it gives appear to be anything but realistic. The advice given by Isaiah in our text is a case-in-point. Who in the world ever could take seriously that statement:

> "Remember not the former things,
> nor consider the things of old.
> Behold I am doing a new thing;
> now it springs forth, do you not
> perceive it?"

How can you wipe out "former things," especially when they are failures and personal blots on your life and record, just because someone recommends it? Even if you would like to, and even if the "recommender" is God?

Memories are not like chalkboards that can be cleaned up with a swipe of an eraser! They are more like granite slabs that have been engraved with a chisel! The past has an incredible tenacity. Once cut in, it hangs on like eternal parts of our beings. So,

> "Remember not the former things,
> nor consider the things of old.
> Behold I am doing a new thing;
> now it springs forth, do you not
> perceive it?"

Do You See What I See?

Come now, Isaiah! Be more realistic!

And if you listen to Jesus, who quoted Isaiah so often, he seems to be taking a similar vein when he gives a group of followers much the same advice:

> *"Truly, I say to you, if you have faith, and never doubt, you will not only do what has been done to the fig tree, but even if you say to this mountain, 'Be taken up and cast into the sea,' it will be done. And whatever you ask in prayer, you will receive, if you have faith."*

So, people are to "remember not" the times they have fallen flat on their faces so often that they have engraved "Loser" on their hearts, and instead get up a head of steam to go out and move mountains simply because they believe they can? Yes, indeed, sometimes the Bible seems to be talking out of the top of its head! You see, there is a whale of a difference between believing and performing! And sometimes the gap between the two seems too broad to be bridged.

One could point out that, though we can *think* we are birds, we can't sprout feathers and fly. Or we could *honestly believe* that we can walk through a brick wall, but that conviction won't protect us when we meet the obstacle head-on.

Yet, that being so, there is no denying that the *attitude* we bring to bear on any situation does have a great deal to do with the success we will have in handling it. The fact is that what people believe they can or cannot do affects profoundly their performance in any venture, regardless of how big or little it is. The individual who approaches a challenging opportunity or problem in life convinced he or she will be a failure, is already doomed before lifting a finger in their own behalf. I have watched that truth operate so often that it is a given in my absolutes for life. Repeatedly, I see people who are in self-made quagmires, unable to move effectively through life because they are haunted by insecurity and fear.

Recently I watched and felt that happen all over again as I stood in a lounge of the psychiatric ward at a local hospital. There before me, distributed around the room, were three patients immobilized by anxiety. They just sat in their chairs and stared into space, unblinking and in total silence. They were so locked up by their fears that they were unable to communicate with anyone, or even move their hands. I often see that same sort of lock-up in less obvious and acute ways outside of places like that. People on the streets, and in the houses and offices that line them, often are uptight and hemmed-in, even when they try to take on the most elementary tasks of living. And what that suggests to each of us, I think, is a haunting lack of confidence in ourselves and in God's power to assist us as we struggle to overcome the obstacles and mountains which confront us all.

We so often fail or bumble through careers and business because we are convinced inside that we haven't got the stuff it takes to succeed.

Marriages too often go sour and homes are too often shattered because couples are convinced that their problems are too big for them to handle.

People sit lonely, without friends, because they think of themselves as duds and as nothings that nobody else could possibly love.

Folks in such straits are found everywhere. They are your friends and mine. Sometimes they are you and me. All are individuals who could be more vibrant, more productive, more fulfilled human beings, but who are in misery because they don't believe they have the power to become the things they dream of being!

And our negative attitudes persist, even though we are surrounded by droves of people, no more able or better equipped than we, who have achieved what seemed to be impossible goals in the face of what looked like impassable mountains. I thought of that while listening to the radio as I drove home from that hospital recently. The announcer was saying that the play *The Miracle Worker* was being revived again. The story of Helen Keller and her teacher Annie Sullivan, it is a rousing portrayal of what a pair of apparently hopeless people were able to accomplish together and individually.

Annie Sullivan, a blind orphan who had been abandoned with her younger brother in a state institution for the insane, was left there to vegetate, stumbling around in its filth and listening to people die. With rats for pets because she had no toys, and with few children to talk to once her brother died, she occupied her hours repeating what the nurses said and did. When night came and the attendants left, Annie practiced what she had learned on the inmates. And with that for her start, she began to build up the skills that eventually got her noticed and opened the way for her transfer to a school for the deaf. There she worked like a spartan to gain the know-how to teach others like herself. She was finally given the chance, as an inexperienced young woman, to go south and take a charge who, when Annie met her, acted more like an animal than a human being.

Helen Keller was not only blind but also deaf and unable to speak. Her parents and the physicians who attended her thought that, at best, the girl from the deaf school could serve as a companion for the youngster. When Annie Sullivan stated that she had come to teach Helen to communicate, Captain Keller's shocked response was, "That's like the blind leading the blind!" "Exactly," retorted Miss Sullivan, "and just you watch how far the two of us can go together!"

The distance they went became legendary! From a frenzied child groping through life because of the personal prison in which her spirit was locked, with the aid of Miss Annie, Helen Keller became a poet, lecturer, humanitarian and inspirer of generations. A person who was once considered an "animal" became the world figure that Kings and Presidents around the world lined up to hear and touch. Uncountable numbers of people, the handicapped and what we call "ordinary people," were drawn to her and inspired to step out on their own. All because of what the faith, and conviction, and effort of a teacher and her pupil accomplished.

I have met others personally who have accomplished much the same thing. They were never celebrated as widely as Helen Keller, but the issues and mountains in their lives were similar.

I watched a man who was forty-six years old, with five children, catch a glimpse of entering the ministry. The problem was that he hadn't even finished high school! But to the amazement of many, he went back and got his diploma, then went on to college and graduated from seminary. What a moving night it was when I helped ordain him and send him on his way as a pastor.

And beside him in my hero book is the "handicapped" boy I sat beside as a college student. He had cerebral palsy and was partially blind. He was so incapacitated that we had to carry him from floor to floor and take turns reading his textbooks to him.

Advent, Christmas, and Epiphany

I still get tingles up my spine when I remember him not only graduating with us, but finishing in the top ten percent of the class when he did! He now owns controlling interest in the business firm that gave him his first job.

And I have seen others who, by all odds, should have been human wrecks. But they got their lives together because of the dogged belief that what appeared to be out of their reach could be attained if they had the faith to set out for their goal.

These people reach such heights not because they have special advantages. Few great people, famous or not, have had an extra boost. Most often they are men and women with the same built-in gifts you and I carry around. What makes them stand out is that they have drawn on the plus of a positive attitude. That has enabled them to unlock their gifts and to "go for it!"

And why not? Psychiatrists have been telling us for a long time that no one uses more than twenty percent of their God-given potential. We all have more in reserve than we show. Once an individual becomes inspired and taps that hidden reservoir, he or she can be propelled forward into making the apparently impossible become a fact. If we plant in our hearts and heads Jesus' promise, we can become more than we have imagined we can!

It is because *fear* chokes off this potential that it is one of our most deadly sins! Nothing insulates against God's coming into our lives as effectively as fear. It is the strongest chain that binds us to the mediocre and tries to convince us that we are losers. That conviction that *we can't advance,* that *we can't grow personally,* that *we are nothings,* that *we must remain as we are,* is one of the worst heresies that hits all mankind!

The Bible tells us that God did not make us to be second rate. He fashioned people from his own image, with the powers to create, and the need for fulfillment in the use of those gifts. And when great dreams come into every heart and head repeatedly throughout life, I am convinced they are God-given and God-desired. And God doesn't want them just thrown aside! When we persuade ourselves, or are persuaded by others, to settle for less than God made us to be, then we shrink the creation that God so lovingly devised when he made you and me!

Do You See What I See?

Remember how young people were always a favorite teaching example for Christ. More than once he cuddled a child to him to illustrate for adults the kind of response he expected them to give him:

> "Unless . . . you become like children, you will never enter the Kingdom of Heaven," he told them.   (Matthew 18:3)

And, as always, the Master had his reasons for saying that, It was his way of reminding us that, in order to reach our spiritual and personal maturity, we must first *recapture the potential of belief* that with his help all things are possible.

Tragically, that is a quality that is too often killed early. But it usually dies only after it is strangled by the pessimism of adults who have had it squeezed out of themselves. In order to preserve or recover that quality, we need to keep our eyes on those unconquered people who have not yet lost it, or with God's help have had it reborn!

The other reason Jesus stressed childhood was that he wanted all of us, youth and oldsters alike, *to renew the all-out trust* that is built into childhood. It is a wonderful kind of faith that makes our little ones put their destinies in our hands without question, believing that what is promised will be done, what is asked will be given, and what is held out to them is guaranteed.

It is that kind of openness that Jesus had in mind when he told us to put our faith in him and become mountain-movers in real life ourselves:

> "Truly I say to you if you have faith and never doubt . . . even if you say to this mountain, 'Be taken up and cast into the sea,' it will be done. And whatever you ask in prayer, you will receive if you have faith."   (Matthew 21:21a, c, 22)

Note the recurrence of the word "faith," in Greek *pistuo,* in this verse. It means "to rely on, to lean on, to bank on utterly." It's opposite, the word "doubt," used in the same passage, is the Greek term *diakrithete*. It means "to be divided in mind, to dispute." Where *pistuo* calls for utterly believing that what Christ says you can do, and be, and have are possible, *diakrithete* makes us discount what he says. *Diakrithete* calls God a liar. It tells us to

Advent, Christmas, and Epiphany

back off on opportunities. It pushes us to put dreams and hopes on the shelf and let them dry up there. It keeps urging us to settle for the short end of life and the disillusionment that inevitably comes.

"Believe" is what our Lord calls us to do! He wants to write into our hearts, while there is still time, that enormous challenges, some looking like mountains to be moved, can be met by us and him together. For those willing to act on his promise, no obstacle, no crisis in living can be so imposing that it cannot be taken on and won! Whether personal problems or world concerns, challenges only become *impossible* for those *who think they are so!*

Once you latch on firmly to the promises of God through Isaiah, and cling to them and the hand of Jesus for dear life, you will learn firsthand that even "mountains" have a way of "flattening out," and new paths into the future come into view. When that happens then "losers" learn how to "win," the impossible occurs, and run-of-the-mill people, like you and I, begin to blossom. For when we take God at his word:

> *"Remember not the former things,*
> *nor consider the things of old.*
> *Behold I am doing a new thing;*
> *now it springs forth . . . ."*

we have taken the step that leads down the road to the "Land of What is Yet to Be," where humankind's and our own, worthiest dreams can come true!

When the Wheels Fall off of Your Life

Epiphany 8   Hosea 2:14-20

"To err is human, to forgive divine," is a proverb with which most of us are familiar. Pointing out, as it does, the obvious truth that where we mortals are fallible God is forgiving, it carries a message with which one can find little to debate.

And yet, while what it says is surely valid, what it does not say, but seems to infer, is another matter. If you read between the lines closely enough, I think you will find the assumption there that forgiveness somehow is an attribute solely of God! If that interlinear reading is accurate, then the proverb is dead wrong! Forgiveness is a human activity that God has equipped us to engage in and commanded us to do. It is not an *option* for life that we are *encouraged* to try.

When God created human beings, he modeled us after himself. Not only did he build into us the marvelous capacities to reason and choose and act. He instilled in us the truly miraculous power to love and pardon one another as he loves and pardons us all. The longer I live, the more I come to understand that God's decision to do that is critical in sustaining life. In order to survive, we must live in a climate of continual forgiveness. Not only must we receive forgiveness from God for ourselves. Without our doing that for one another, this planet, and each of us who inhabit it, would simply explode!

No one understood that better than Hosea. He had watched his nation repeatedly run to God for help, and receive it, for everything from rain for draught-stricken crops to aid fending off invading armies. He stood by, after the big-heartedness of God had answered their prayers, and watched the people just blessed turn and shun that same open-eared God as though he were a plague. (Hosea 11:1ff)

Jesus understood the need for forgiveness, too, and saw the need for it nearly everywhere he looked. So great an importance did he attach to changing the vindictive snarls that peppered the folks he moved among that he pointed to it often. He reserved a large block of his preaching to stress our need to forgive our thorns in the flesh, especially those whom we so often label publicly, or in secret, as our enemies.

In his Sermon on the Mount, Jesus lined out the principle that we are "to love our enemies," "bless those who persecute us," and "pray for those who despitefully use us," as foolish as that advice seems on the face of it. In some of his block-buster parables, like the Prodigal Son, and the Unforgiving Servant, Jesus kept hammering home this same theme. The bottom line in each of the stories was that it is not just *commendable* to forgive; it is *mandatory*. In fact, *God* will not forgive *us* if *we* do not forgive *each other!*

To make sure that even the most dense of us would get the point, he gave us, in the eighteenth chapter of Matthew, his story about the forgiven debtor who in turn refused to do the same for a brother. (Matthew 18:23-35) Catching us all by the necks, he shakes us to get our attention, then says, "What happened to him can happen to you! Do you want God to lower the boom for all you have done in the past, and on which he has the record in hand? If not, then tear up the foreclosure notes you are so eager to deliver on the people you have over the barrel!"

> *"For so your heavenly Father will do to every one of you, if you do not forgive your brother from your heart."*
>
> (Matthew 18:35)

Advent, Christmas, and Epiphany

There it is, bill-board high and clear as crystal from both Hosea and Jesus himself! You and I, not just God, must forgive. Forgiveness, like erring, is human, too. What I want to do this morning is deal with *how we can get on with the often painful, and always difficult task of doing that!* Too often we are left with *demands* by preachers, who are long on diagnosis and short on prescriptions.

What I have learned, in a continuing struggle to do what Jesus orders, is that the first step in the forgiveness process is to admit to ourselves that *there are people against whom we hold spite,* and whom we detest or hate because of the pain that they have caused us. Until we can do that, nothing constructive can really get under way.

That sounds like so simple a step to take that it is hardly worth mentioning. But the fact is that it is an excruciatingly difficult thing for Christians, and particularly "church people," to do. Most of the time we walk around *denying that we even have such negative and hostile feelings.* Why, we love everybody! Nothing they do really hurts us! Oh, we just brush off their barbs as though nothing had occurred! All because we feel pressed to put on those polite exteriors, even though inside our emotional pots are boiling and we are seething with resentment!

For too long we have even put a premium on such phoney behavior. The ideal Christian is the one with the perpetual grin and the eternal "all is just beautiful with me" air about them. If they need a patron saint it could well be one of our own citizens, who kept telling the world so often that it became his trademark: "I never met a man I didn't like."

I remember asking my grandfather about that line when I heard it on a recording that he had of Will Rogers. "How can he have liked everybody? Didn't he ever meet the mean ones?" I asked him. "As big a star as he was he had to meet plenty of them," he said from behind his newspaper. "It's just that Will Rogers liked to lie a lot!"

Maybe the real reason that Rogers said that was that he had trouble dealing with his feelings. Or maybe he had a public image he had to keep intact. He met some people he would have been sick not to have disliked . . . like Al Capone, and Huey Long, and the Imperial Wizard of the Ku Klux Klan, and a host of others like them who crossed his path on his world travels!

Do You See What I See?

But, then, most of us have a hard time coming clean with ourselves. And the closer and more intimate the relationship, the more wrenching it is to admit the grudges we hold, and the more deeply we try to bury them. When such people cut us, instead of dealing with the wound, even while it is bleeding, we put a cast on it to hide it! The result is that underneath it festers and stays inflamed, if out of sight. Given time, the wounds finally burst, frequently at unexpected moments and with a fury we have trouble understanding.

All of us walk through most of our lives infected by such gashes. We go around carrying chips on our shoulders without knowing how they ever got there! We get as tight as stretched garters beneath our veneers, and don't know why. We sense something inside of us is all snarled up, but we have camouflaged it for so long that it has become like a ghost that haunts us and controls us, always from the shadows.

If we are going to change that, *we need to turn and face the monster.* We need to *name it, own it,* and *admit* that it is there. Every human being has been racked by another so hard that the scar of the act is still present and tender. Before we can treat it, we first must be willing to open it up to the light. There *are* people *we hate* . . . as there are people *who hate us!* That's where the cure begins.

The second step in the forgiveness process is to *change vantage points with the offender.* About as hard to do as owning our feelings, it requires that we try to understand what it was that triggered the pain in the first place. What makes this move so gruesome is that we usually don't want to understand the **actions** of our adversaries. There is the fear that if we saw all that was involved, we might ease off on some of the guilt we make them bear for what they did to us. That might let them off of the hook on which we want to keep them!

This is a well-founded fear! If we could see into their lives, you and I might be a lot less hateful than we are. There are often loads they carry that would make anyone hostile. The problem is that they are hidden from the gaze of the casual observer.

It is something like the experience I had as a teenager when I went to a physician's office. I had broken an ankle sliding into a

Advent, Christmas, and Epiphany

base in a ball game. When the cast was taken off, I had to appear for a final examination before I could rejoin the team. The office was located on the seventh floor of a building across the street from a huge church which I had walked past hundreds of times before that visit. An enormous Gothic structure, I had often admired the carvings on its stone facade, but that day I saw something that I never had guessed was there.

From the window in the waiting room, I looked out on the Cathedral's roof and towers. Between two tall belfries were a pair of huge chimneys carved with lace-work, just like the bell towers. On top of the stone caps that finished them were the final decorations which the artists had chiseled . . . five square crosses cut deeply into the rims, resting like a crown on their heads.

From the streets below, no one could see those crosses on the tops of the chimneys. From the pavement, everything seemed to be soaring up into the sky, free and easy. Only from the vantage point denied to the crowds of pedestrians could one see the symbols of pain nestling there in the midst of the glory!

The lives of those at whom our hostilities are pointed, often bear crosses we can't know exist. And some of those crosses are ones we may have carved there with actions and words we shot in their direction. We often are responsible for other people's actions toward us! If we knew what they had to contend with, we might be less judgmental and more compassionate.

This is not to say that we should blame all the destructive things people do on the burdens they have to bear! They, like we, are accountable for the damage done to others. That is where *true guilt* comes home to roost! But the quick condemnation we render, the laying in wait for the day and occasion when we will have the chance to even old scores, or do them one better, could be defused. And that would be a healing experience for us as well as for them.

The third step that forgiveness takes for me is *praying for those who caused the grief which I rock,* and *nurse,* and *pamper* with a vengeance! Of all of the steps that are needed to air our hate, this has been for me the hardest to learn to do. I have listened to Jesus saying to the disciples, and through them to us: "Pray for those who despitefully use you and persecute you." (Matthew 5:44)

Do You See What I See?

I used to feel that he was off the wall with a piece of advice that no human being ought to be given. To do that required that I think about the individual who hurt me . . . and call them back into mind when I would rather forget them, permanently! To bring them back dragged with them the event that had caused the problem in the first place.

With the passing of the years, and the maturity they have brought, I have come to learn how indispensable this step really is! *Bringing enemies close forces me to stay in touch with them,* as painful as that can be. I don't know about you, but that forces me to keep seeing them as *human beings,* fallible like myself. And it is harder and harder to keep the hate factor high when, in cataloging *their* misdeeds, I have to remember my own! In touching them *as people,* they frequently begin to fade as *enemies.*

A relative of mine had an experience like that during the Battle of the Bulge in World War II. He was part of the American force positioned to repel the German attempt to break through the Allied offensive. As he moved through a heavily-wooded area one night, the Germans opened up with artillery on the advancing U.S. troops.

The battle had been at such close quarters before the darkness settled that, when it fell, he couldn't remember which way his own troop lines were. He looked for a shell hole where he could sit out the barrage. He saw a crater a little ahead of him, and running for all that he was worth, he jumped in . . . and landed on top of a German soldier!

He had fallen on the fellow so that the German's arms were pinned against the ground and he couldn't move. As quick as a flash, my relative reached back and pulled out his bayonet. He raised his hand to plunge the blade into the man who lay beneath him, when a flare burst overhead, lighting up the whole area. That light made him look squarely into the face of the man he was about to kill.

That was the first time he had been that close to a live German soldier in combat. Just that day before he had shot two enemy troops off of a motor cycle as they raced down a road. They had been about fifty yards from him. All he could remember as he pulled the trigger of his rifle was how funny it looked as they flew through the air, their cycle going in one direction and their bodies in another.

But never before had he felt the warm flesh of a man's chin under the palm of his hand as he pushed his head back preparing to kill him. Never had he had to look that man full in the eyes. And when he did, he couldn't bring down that bayonet. It was as though his arm had frozen in the snow.

"I just sat there for a long moment," he said. "And then I slowly slid back off of the fellow, and slumped against the back of the shell hole. The German raised his head and stared at me. Almost without thinking, my hand went up to my shirt pocket, and I pulled out a cigarette and handed it to him. I tossed over my Zippo, and watched his shaking hands as he lit it. For the next two hours the war was over for us. We sat in the snow of the crater and used the light of the exploding shells and flares to show each other pictures of our families, and talk about what it is to spend Christmas at home, and what plans each of us had for the day the hostilities would be over."

Before dawn, when the bombardment had ended, the two shook hands. Then they jumped out of that shell hole and each went in his own direction. Though they had come together as warriors, in the midst of the raging hell of conflict each had learned that even the enemy is a person.

The contact that prayer forces on us, even in the midst of conflict, can do the very same thing for us, if we give ourselves to it. Prayer puts us into the same shell hole with our enemy. Seeing the enemy as a mirror into which we are looking can help squelch the forces of hate. For if *God dealt with us* like *we are driven to deal with each other,* where would *both of us be* when the carnage was over?

God reached out to his people with *encircling arms* instead of with a club, or worse. No vindictive furor. No eternal turning of the divine back. Instead:

> ". . . behold, I will allure her,
>   and bring her into the
>   wilderness,
>   and speak tenderly to her.

Do You See What I See?

> *And there I will give her*
>   *vineyards,*
> *and make the Valley of Achor a door*
>   *of hope.*
> *And there she shall answer as in the*
>   *days of her youth,*
> *as at the time when she came out of*
>   *the land of Egypt."*

The broken bonds between us and him were to be healed. That mode is one he wants to see developed in our lives and passed on to those who have hurt and betrayed us as we have him. Going through life, taking one person after the other by the neck, trying to squeeze from them payment in spades for their sins against us ends up as potential suicide as well as possible murder. For, you see, hatred and vengeance are at least as consuming for those who hold them as for those against whom they are unleashed. They lock people up tighter than any dungeon, and keep them there to grow bitter, and finally shrivel inside, and die. To save us all from that, Hosea reminds us that forgiveness is the one God-inspired key that can pop open that lock on our lives. As Shakespeare wrote of it:

> *"The quality of mercy is not strain'd.*
>   *It droppeth as the gentle rain from*
>   *heaven*
> *Upon the place beneath. It is twice blessed:*
>   *It blesseth him that gives and him that*
>   *takes."*
>   *(The Merchant of Venice,* Act IV, Scene 1)

May it come as a torrent into your erring life and mine.

"Help! Help! Help!"

The Transfiguration of Our Lord   2 Kings 2:1-12a

In the stage play, *The Tea House of the August Moon,* an Okinowan servant named Sakini trots out onto the stage, bows low to the audience, then begins a monologue giving his philosophy of life. Speaking as though he were oblivious to the audience, Sakini thoughtfully makes this observation: "Suffering makes me think. Thinking makes men wise. And wisdom makes life bearable." Though buried in the midst of the rest of what he says, his observation is one profound enough to bear remembering, even if it is not what we would like to hear about living, even from a character in a play!

What Sakini talks about right up front is such a universal issue of life that none of us can escape it. Pain, in one form or another, touches the whole spectrum of the human family, from Sakini to Elisha to us! Whether it is the loss of a friend or loved one (as Elisha experienced when Elijah was swept out of his life), or bodily breakdowns, or relationship fractures that cave our hearts in and start the blood flowing, suffering is something with which I, like you all, have to deal with constantly, not only as a Pastor but as an individual, and a father, and a husband, and as a friend.

Over the years, I have taken it on in nearly every degree of its impact. Looking into my own mirror, as well as into the faces

Do You See What I See?

of the people who come to me in all sorts of disarray from pain and grief, my constant challenge has been to try to understand why it is that we have to endure such jolts in our lives.

All of you have been in places where adversity has touched you and yours, as it has touched me and mine. I am just as certain that, when we have tried to make some sense out of it, not all of us have come to the same conclusions about what it all means.

Some folks I know have used the fact of suffering to discard any concept of sanity in the fabric of life. If they had to make the kind of statement Sakini did about what they think of living, they would trot out on the stage to look at us and say: "Suffering makes people hurt. Hurting makes people hopeless. Hopelessness makes life heartless and cruel."

Pain really can appear to be another piece in the puzzle of existence whose parts seem purposely cut so that they never fit together in a way that makes any real sense. Like Shakespeare says in *Macbeth*, taken on the whole, life looks like ". . . a tale told by an idiot, full of sound and fury, signifying nothing." (Act V, Scene 5)

And at given moments I think they have the issue by the right end! I have to admit that I have agreed with them at various stages in my life, and still verge on doing so during some of my most intense and prolonged suffering. As I come up against a pain-racked individual who cannot get well, and yet cannot seem to die, and others who outwardly *are healthy but who want* intensely to die, existence does seem to be a cruel and heartless a thing. I have wondered how God can be real and not do something to pull the plug on such suffering, on the spot! Some kinds of pain seem to be utterly dead-ended and purposeless.

I remember first hitting that kind of suffering head-on when I walked into a room in a children's wing of a hospital. I heard a baby crying as I went down the corridor past its room. When I stopped, and then stepped inside the door, I saw the infant. It was no more than seven-to-nine months old, with a head the size of a small basketball and a tumor on its back about the size of a grapefruit. It was lying on its stomach whimpering in pain. As I moved to its crib and stood there looking down at it in shock, a voice came from the wall behind me: "Well Father, what do you have to say about that?"

Advent, Christmas, and Epiphany

I turned to see the baby's father leaning against the door jam with tears in his eyes. "What does your God have in his bag for a dying baby? My God died long ago. This little one of ours is not going to make it to a year of age and yet his life will be gone with nothing more to it than this." Choked up myself, I stood there in silence as he turned and walked down the hallway, leaving me beside the tiny bed.

This past week I sat beside another baby, eighteen months old and dying of inoperable lung disease. I realized that after a quarter century of experience, prayer, and being belted around myself, I still don't have the answer to what I experienced in those rooms, or in many other places of anguish, all wrapped up and neatly answered by some theological or philosophical formula!

Still . . . when some kinds of pain have come to pummel my life and home as they have yours, the bruises and breaks they have left have done more than fill me with terror and bewilderment and fury. They have brought some things to the surface of my life that have taught me about myself and existence at large, and how God fit into both. Those moments of suffering have helped me glimpse, even if fleetingly at times, how pain has helped clean up my life and often, but not always, burned away some of the ignorance that has put space between me and other human beings.

What some times of trial have shown me is the enormous potential that exists within pain to take the starch out of our hearts, and make them expandable. It has demonstrated its power to retune the strings of those same hearts so that they can vibrate to the hurts and disappointments of others. In a way that is absolutely unique, pain has the ability to make each of us become participating parts of the human race. It does that by making us more capable of having compassion for others who are bleeding and bruised, too.

I have learned that we can never reach the fullness of our maturity without the growth factor of pain, in one form or another. We *must* have heartaches, frustration, disappointment, loss, fear, yes, and even illness, if we are to understand and help other persons who face them, just as we need them for ourselves. These traditional "demons" drive us to come to *know ourselves,* and *our dependency* on God and one another, as nothing else has the power to do.

Do You See What I See?

It isn't easy to concede, even to ourselves, that these "plagues" may have any gifts to leave behind for us. When Shakespeare says: "Sweet are the uses of adversity" we don't know whether to first have him committed to an institution or stone him! When events go thunderously against us, it is difficult to face the fact that in the anguish of the storm there actually can be *purpose,* and *needed lessons to learn,* within the ache and sorrow.

"It has done me good," said William Wordsworth Longfellow, "to be somewhat parched by the heat and drenched by the rain of life."

"A smooth sea never made a skillful mariner," said an author whose name has been forgotten before his observation has.

"Affliction comes to us all," said Henry Ward Beecher, "Not to make us sad, but sober. Not to make us sorry but wise."

It is, as Isaiah said to the people of Israel during the midst of the most intense suffering the Jews endured until the death camps of Hitler: "Behold I have refined you, I have chosen you in the furnace of affliction." (Isaiah 48:10) And those who heard that, as have many who have read it, learned that what Isaiah said rings true. It is in the "furnace of affliction," in those moments that bring suffering, that we find where our strengths and weaknesses are. The "blessing" that suffering often leaves in its wake is the power it has to *enhance that strength,* and *turn that weakness into sensitivity* and *compassion.*

I don't know about you, but in my experience, both with others and myself, I have found that pain has been the needed catalyst to help bring *narrow mindedness,* and *hard heartedness,* and *"me firstism"* to heal. It has also enabled me to see that it is most often those who have never been singed by the "flames," or who have never had to long for help, or who never cried because they felt lost or finished, who are the folks who lack pity or the quick willingness to reach out to those in need. It has driven me to the conclusion that it is those who have scars of their own who are the ones you can count on to rush in to help bind up the wounds that life inflicts. Suffering has helped make them the helpers and healers of the world.

Advent, Christmas, and Epiphany

In his play, *The Angel That Troubled The Waters,* Thornton Wilder presents a character who, infected with life-long pain, grumbles to an Angel about what a drawback his infirmity has been: "It is no shame to boast to an Angel of what I might . . . do in love's service were I freed from this bondage." With a sensitive look the Angel slowly shakes his head: "Without your wound, where would your power be? The very angels themselves cannot persuade the wretched and blundering children on earth as can one human being broken on the wheels of living." (Quoted in *The Cross of Hosea,* H. Wheeler Robinson, p. 30.)

That is true, I think. Without our wounds, where would our power be, yours and mine? It is often in those wounds that our power to understand, and love and raise one another up have their source. They are absolutely precious, these wounds, and the wisdom and compassion they bring. They are precious, indeed, because the price for gaining both usually has been staggering!

But not all people gain something positive, or grow from, suffering, even a little. Some individuals never learn any more from it than they do from any other experiences in life. Its positive potential is missed because *they never probe its nature.* Instead, they take the short and easier route in dealing with grief. They simply become embittered and hateful because of what they endure. Suffering makes them turn sour and vicious on life, and even on God.

Peter De Vries describes such a person in his novel, *The Blood of the Lamb.* It is the story of a father whose life is shaken when his eleven-year-old daughter develops leukemia and slowly begins to lose her battle for life. The tale reaches a climax on the day the little girl is to celebrate her birthday.

Her father sets out for his daily visit with a beautifully decorated cake under his arm, so that his daughter and her roommates can celebrate the great day in the hospital ward. On his way, the father stops at a church to pray for his little one's recovery. While he is kneeling in prayer, a nurse rushes in to tell him that Carol has contracted another infection and has begun to slip away. With his heart pounding, he runs from the church to reach his baby before her eyes close. In the pew still sits the cake which his housekeeper had so lovingly decorated for a happy day.

Do You See What I See?

A few hours later, with Carol dead, and his mind ripped with grief, the father stumbles back into the church. Going up the aisle, he picks up the parcel he had left behind. Then, half staggering, he heads for the exit.

As he reaches the top of the stairs leading to the street, he looks up and sees hanging above the doorway a huge crucifix. What he sees nailed to it is the One who had not stopped the death of his child! In his frenzy of anger, he tears the cake from the box, and with all of the strength he can muster, hurls it squarely into the face of the Man on the Cross. Then, with tears of bitterness running down his cheeks, he stands before the figure and watches as the pieces of pastry, intended to celebrate life, fall to the ground from the thorn-crowned head.

Not just fictional fathers, but real life ones, as well as real life mothers, and children, and even you and I, can respond to suffering like that! Who hasn't, on occasion, hurled our hurt into the face of God and said, "There! Take that, you forsaking monster!" Suffering has the potential to "knee jerk" us into counter attacking it like that.

But I have seen others deal with it in a vastly different way. Hit by experiences that were enormously painful, their reactions set a different tone for their lives. When tragedy whacked them, they used it as the reshaper of lives that are now richer than before.

I can still see in my mind's eye a young mother, stricken with multiple sclerosis, who with a family of four children, aged three to eleven, begins to lose her facilities. And I am on hand as she begins to train them to keep house, and with her husband, to learn to care more fully for one another and themselves. And just days before she dies, as I sit beside her wheelchair, giving her what will be her last earthly Communion, I can still hear her telling me: "What a wonderful gift of a close knit family we have been given because of what has come."

And I think of Paul Van Buren, a former contributor to *The Lutheran* magazine, whose son was afflicted with cerebral palsy. I once watched him as he tenderly cared for the boy, who required constant care for many years before he died. And I shall remember for as long as I live Paul saying that, if there must be such children, he is happy God gave him one, because he knew how to love him.

They, along with armies of other people who have had their heads "bloodied but unbowed," have been *ennobled by* suffering rather than *crushed* by it. That has happened because they have been able to see, and use, grief as a springboard to bounce high enough out of their pits to see life from the top of the arc which that flight gave them. And from that vantage point, they glimpsed the truth that Jesus shared with his disciples on a night when he was to suffer some of his greatest pain: "I say to you, unless a grain of wheat falls into the earth and dies, it remains alone; but if it dies, it bears much fruit." (John 12:24)

As much as we wish it were not so, some parts of us must die if new and greater dimensions of our being are to be set free. Like a caterpillar bursting its cocoon, the pain of the struggle is the prelude to the flight toward new levels of life not possible in the isolation of "grieflessness." Our wounds and our losses give us our power to do that, making Ralph Waldo Emerson right on the mark when he wrote: "Whilst [a man] sits on the cushion of advantage he goes to sleep. When he is pushed, tormented, defeated, he has a chance to learn something."

That is precisely where Elisha found himself that day by the Jordan. Pushed and tormented, left staring up into heaven as his Master Elijah was whooshed away, he was alone, and heavyhearted. But as Elijah faded from sight, the *grief* and *fear* held also a chance *to learn something* that would carry Elisha through all the trials and tribulations his life would hold. That something was this . . . that the same God who sent his "chariot and horsemen" to take care of Elijah would stand ready to "swing low" to stand by Elisha as well.

And the very same thing will hold true for us, too. Just you wait and see.